About Access Archaeology

Access Archaeology offers a different publishing model for specialist academic material that might traditionally prove commercially unviable, perhaps due to its sheer extent or volume of colour content, or simply due to its relatively niche field of interest. This could apply, for example, to a PhD dissertation or a catalogue of archaeological data.

All *Access Archaeology* publications are available in open-access e-pdf format and in print format. The open-access model supports dissemination in areas of the world where budgets are more severely limited, and also allows individual academics from all over the world the opportunity to access the material privately, rather than relying solely on their university or public library. Print copies, nevertheless, remain available to individuals and institutions who need or prefer them.

The material is refereed and/or peer reviewed. Copy-editing takes place prior to submission of the work for publication and is the responsibility of the author. Academics who are able to supply print-ready material are not charged any fee to publish (including making the material available in open-access). In some instances the material is type-set in-house and in these cases a small charge is passed on for layout work.

Our principal effort goes into promoting the material, both in open-access and print, where *Access Archaeology* books get the same level of attention as all of our publications which are marketed through e-alerts, print catalogues, displays at academic conferences, and are supported by professional distribution worldwide.

Open-access allows for greater dissemination of academic work than traditional print models could ever hope to support. It is common for an open-access e-pdf to be downloaded hundreds or sometimes thousands of times when it first appears on our website. Print sales of such specialist material would take years to match this figure, if indeed they ever would.

This model may well evolve over time, but its ambition will always remain to publish archaeological material that would prove commercially unviable in traditional publishing models, without passing the expense on to the academic (author or reader).

Egil's Saga:

Traditional evidence for Brúnanburh compared to Literary, Historic and Archaeological Analyses

John R. Kirby

Access Archaeology

Archaeopress Publishing Ltd
Summertown Pavilion
18-24 Middle Way
Summertown
Oxford OX2 7LG

www.archaeopress.com

ISBN 978-1-78969-109-2
ISBN 978-1-78969-110-8 (e-Pdf)

© Archaeopress and J R Kirby 2019

Cover image: Egil Skallagrimsson. From the 17th century Icelandic manuscript AM 426 fol., Árni Magnússon Institute in Iceland. (http://en.wikipedia.org/wiki/Image:Egil_Skallagrimsson_17c_manuscript.jpg)

Printed and bound in Great Britain by
Marston Book Services Ltd, Oxfordshire

All rights reserved. No part of this book may be reproduced, stored in retrieval system, or transmitted, in any form or by any means, electronic, mechanical, photocopying or otherwise, without the prior written permission of the copyright owners.

This book is available direct from Archaeopress or from our website www.archaeopress.com

Dedicated to my wife and daughter

This research into the Battle of Brúnanburh and Egil's Saga was commenced after the death of my elder cousin in a car accident in 1969. My family came from Northern England, went to Castle Hedingham, Essex and then to the East Midlands. I came to Egil's Saga late in life and this enabled me to pursue the subject in greater depth.

ACKNOWLEDGEMENTS

My wife and daughter have been long suffering and most understanding of my research, but it was my mother who first stirred an interest in the origins of both families, coupled with other curious events, meeting various people who became friends, some of whom seemed to know about my family.

There are many people I wish to acknowledge over the years, many of whom have died. Yet, they all have the virtuous characteristics of friendship in common plus a disposition to impart learning, understanding and care. These people I regard as my friends and count myself lucky to have encountered them in my life: Dr John and Mary Blomfield, Andrew and May Bland, Nell Bland, Wilfred and Juliet Howard, William 'Bill' Morris, Hon. Patrick Lindsay, Paul and Elizabeth Richardson, Dr Andree Porter, Christopher Dark, Prof. Paul and Marline Ewert, Rev. Dr David and Dr Megan Price, Prof. David Taggart, Prof. Chris Gosden, Emeritus Prof. Gary Lock, Prof. Roger Tomlin, Emeritus Prof. David Blackman, Prof. Martin Henig, Magnus Magnusson, Gillian Fellows-Jensen, Prof. Peter Foote, Prof. Raymond Page, Emeritus Prof. Michael Barnes, Prof. Ursula Dronke and Dr Richard Perkins. There are many others I have not mentioned, some I hold close.

I would like to thank the following institutions, Birmingham University Edgbaston, Birmingham Art College, BBC Birmingham (Broad St & Pebble Mill), the Bodleian Library, Oxford University English Faculty Library, Oxford University Archaeological Institute, Oxford University Department for Continuing Education, Leicestershire Records Office, Barrow in Furness Records Office, the National Archives at Kew and the College of Arms.

Lastly, when I least expected it, completely out of the blue, for their most gracious help and funding I am indebted to the Ancient World Research Cluster, Wolfson College, Oxford.

Egil's Saga:
Traditional evidence for Brúnanburh compared to Literary, Historic and Archaeological Analyses

John R. Kirby

CONTENTS

INTRODUCTION	5
RAISON D'ÊTRE	5
SNORRI'S CHARACTER AND HISTORICAL BACKGROUND	6
HISTORICAL ANALYSIS OF THE LITERARY EVIDENCE	7
PAGAN RITUAL CONTRASTED TO EARLY CHRISTIAN BELIEFS	15
HISTORICAL AND ARCHAEOLOGICAL EVIDENCE	18
THE SOCIO-RELIGIOUS SPHERE	21
PRIOR TO 'THE GREAT BATTLE'	26
THE CHRISTIAN BEHAVIOUR OF ÆTHELSTAN	33
THE FYLDE: THE PLAIN OF DEATH	35
THE 'PATHS OF THE DEAD'	36
GENEALOGICAL EVIDENCE - Jarl Gunnar Hlífrsson's family relationship with Thorsteinn Egilsson	41
MARITIME AND LANDSCAPE SUMMARY IN THE BRÚNANBURH MSS	44
APPENDIX A - Christian Relationships in Iceland and England	49
CHRONOLOGY	50
BIBLIOGRAPHY	54

List of Illustrations

Figure 1. The Sculpture in Urswick Church.. 20
Figure 2. Kirkby Hall, Furness.. 20
Figure 3. 1580-90 Map of Furness.. 21
Figure 4. British Library. MS Baptism of Rollo... 31
Figure 5. Æthelstan's Continental Links... 32
Figure 6. Battle Triangle.. 35
Figure 7. Hand drawn inscription of Thored's Holybook.. 39
Figure 8. Facsimile of Thored's MS... 40
Figure 9. Genealogical analysis.. 43
Figure 10. Dalesfolk Names in Southern Cumbria... 46
Figure 11. Amounderness.. 47

Egil's Saga: Traditional evidence for Brúnanburh compared to Literary, Historic and Archaeological Analyses

John R. Kirby

INTRODUCTION

The Saga. Although regarded as a family saga, the style of *Egil's Saga Skalla-Grímssonar* is Homeric rather than Hesiodic Such a refinement indicates that individuals have added to and created a type of 'literary palimpsest', embellished the 'hero' (a dark, violent poet) and content owing to its oral inheritance. [*Nordal, S. (ed) 1933; see also MSS AM162 A fol θ (mid 13th century); though the chief MS: Möðruvallabók [M] AM132 fol., Reykjavík (14th century) was employed by Bjarni Einarsson 2003*]. Thus, it raises problems not only for the Saga but also for the veracity of the *Brúnanburh* context (AD 937). Unlike *Höensa Þorirs Saga*[1], which is Hesiodic in style, simple evidence has not been embroidered or aggrandized it retains its original format. Therefore, on this basis Egil's Saga cannot be regarded as an historical work[2] for its style is semi-fictional prose with skáldic verse - *dróttkvætt*, it becomes a type of 'genre fiction', slanting towards a novel, an early 'Scandinavian Noir'.

Romantic and political ideals of the past Age prevail; they affect the present and can disturb historical accuracy; even the authenticity of this saga can be questioned for it was collated three centuries after the events portrayed. Torfi H. Túlunius[3] describes a framework to verify the narrative, "a more dynamic way, a generic system organised by five principles: genealogy, geography, (both spatio-temporal and concrete), the others are religion, the supernatural and social status". For Torfi's structure does not ignore but rather compliments Sigurður Nordal's[4] 'time' categorization of prose: *samtidssagaer* (contemporary time's sagas describing events in the time range of composition), *fortidssagaer* (olden time's sagas AD 850-1100) and *öldtidssagaer* (ancient sagas before the settlement of Iceland); interestingly, Túlunius' 'elemental' framework may illuminate differences inherent in Egil's Saga. The article reconsiders the paradigm.

RAISON D'ÊTRE

Therefore, the author separates Túlunius' two areas – (a) the spatio-temporal / concrete and (b) the paranormal / fantastic in the saga, to verify reality from weird for a conceptual framework. What results is most interesting for it demonstrates the 'mishmash' of events and images creating 'Form' in Egil's Saga.[5]

[1.] Morris, W. & Magnusson, E.1903 *Höensa Þórirs Saga. (The Saga of Hen Thorir)*. Cincinnati, Ohio: Byway Press.

[2.] See Einarsson Bjarni 2003 *Egil's Saga*. Saga Book. Vol. XXVII. Viking Society for Northern Research. U.C. L. He describes the 'histgraphy of the conflated MSS'.

[3.] Torfi H. Túlunius 2000. "An Attempt at Application: Interpreting Egils saga." *The Matter of the North. The Rise of Literary Fiction in Thirteenth Century Iceland.* Transl. Randi C. Eldevik. Odense: Odense University Press, pp 234-89. 529.

[4.] Nordal, Sigurður. (ed) 1933 *Egil's Saga Skalla-Grimssonar*, Islendk Fornrit ii, Reykjavik. p181; see also Oskar Bandle (Ed) 2002. *The Nordic Languages* Handbücher zur Sprach- und Kommunikations-wissenschaft. An International Handbook of the History of North Germanic Languages.Vol 1. Band 22.1, Walter de Gruyter. Berlin. Pages 824-5, 832). This is not to diminish Nordal's valuable work of 'time' categorization of prose but to analyse the conceptual framework underpinning the saga.

[5.] Egil's Saga was collated c. AD 1242/3.

This article confirms various incongruities within the above areas highlighting that the veracity accorded by some scholars, who hold the accuracy of this saga as absolute, must be treated with extreme caution. While different family lineages and social aspects are discussed, one was found to be skewed in the saga. Is there reciprocity in the story for the traditions of *Brúnanburh* when compared to historical sources? If distinct mismatches can be shown through historical, geographical and genealogical sources then we have no alternative but to disregard Egil's Saga as a material source for Brúnanburh. Yet, conversely these incongruities can validate correct events.

SNORRI'S CHARACTER AND HISTORICAL BACKGROUND

Guðrún Nordal's post-graduate lecture (1991-2)[6] in the Scandinavian Studies Department at University College London of 'Snorri the Man' *(c.AD 1179-23rd September 1241, aet 62)* demonstrated a number of aspects of his character: Snorri's private life; the chieftain; the Sturlungs and Snorri's killing. Importantly, Guðrún describes Snorri's timeline,

1179	born, son of *Guðný Böðvarsdóttir* and *Sturla Þórðarson at Dalasýsla, Iceland*.
1181	fostered at Oddi by *Jón Loftsson*.
1199	married to *Herdís Bersadóttir*; they lived at Oddi.
1202	they move to Borg á Mýrum.
1206	Snorri moves to Reykjaholt; *Herdís* stays on at Borg.
1215-18	Snorri a lawspeaker.
1218-20	Snorri in Norway; stays with *earl Skúli* (*lendr maðr*).
1222	partnership with *Hallveig Ormsdóttir*.
1222-31	Snorri a lawspeaker.
1237-39	Snorri in Norway with *earl Skúli*. Goes to Iceland in spite of *King Hákon's* ban.
1241	*Hallveig Ormsdóttir* dies.
23/09/1241	Snorri killed in Reykjaholt by *Gizzurr Þórvaldsson's* men: *Markús Marðarson, Simon Knútr, Àrni Beiskr, Þórsteinn Guðinason,* and *Þórarinn Àsgrimsson* were with *Gizzurr Þórvaldsson* but *Àrni Beiskr* (the Bitter) gave Snorri his death blow.

This article suggests that Egil's Saga may have been collated in note form c. AD 1220 – 1231 by Snorri but according to the literary time-structure of specific words and phrases the saga was probably constructed and added too much later – an historic/literary palimpsest. Further, there are certain literary aspects described in the first person that could not have happened to Egil at that time. These structural literary aspects can be assessed and dated, thus giving validity to the argument that Snorri may not have written the Saga in its first redaction. Further, some historical aspects are incorrect.

[6] Guðrún Nordal is the daughter of Sigurður Nordal. This timeline extract was taken from her PostGraduate lecture in the Scandinavian Studies Dept at UCL. Her CV states: "Guðrún started her research career in London, after graduating from Oxford in 1988. She was appointed a lecturer at University College London in 1990. She moved to Iceland then was awarded a postdoc position from the Icelandic Research Council in 1993, and was appointed a senior research fellow at the Arni Magnusson Manuscript Insititute in 1997. In 2001 she was appointed an associate professor at the University of Iceland, and has been a professor since 2005. In 2009 she became the director of the Arni Magnusson Institute for Icelandic Studies".

Was there some information about *Brúnanburh* from the marriage of *Thorstein Egilsson* and *Iófríð Gunnarsdóttir* in the library at Oddi or Borg that Snorri had read or inherited? On the basis of probability, there appears to have been so. Snorri was fostered and educated at Oddi by Jón Loftsson and would have had access to Jón's books of Greek and Latin. Jón Loftsson was educated at *Kungahälla* in *Bohuslän* which was the capital centre of Norway at that time. Jón's maternal grandfather was King Magnus the III of Norway.

Snorri is noted mainly as an historian and poet but he was also a lawyer, twice becoming lawspeaker at the Althing and also a politician. It was this latter aspect that brought about his death. For Snorri pursued a course of intrigue with the Norwegian *King Hákon Hákonarson IV* that was contrary to the interests of those senior chieftains in Iceland. *King Hákon* had plans of unifying Iceland with his realm of Norway and Snorri supported a union with Norway. To tempt Snorri *Hákon* made him a squire (*skutilsvein*) of the king's court with a prospect of becoming the jarl of Iceland under *Hákon's* jurisdiction. Snorri was ambitious and unfortunately 'rubbed people up the wrong way'. He also had an eye for women and was regarded in some quarters as a philanderer which did not endear him to many people. However, it was his political intriguing that was to bring about his death. After a certain amount of feuding with other chieftains, a small civil war resulted in Iceland between those that wanted union with Norway and those who wanted a republic. Because of this and the fact that Snorri had gone back to Iceland against *Hákon's* command troubles mounted for Snorri. Therefore, *Hákon* aligned himself with *Gizzurr Þórvaldsson* Snorri's son-in-law and nemesis.

HISTORICAL ANALYSIS OF THE LITERARY EVIDENCE

Stylistic development in the Saga. The Northern prose of Egil's Saga has a parallel to the 'Homeric' or 'Epic' style demonstrating a possible Greek derivation in its construction. Could Snorri Sturlusson and other contemporary writers have been aware of Homer (c. 8th-7th century), Hesiod (c. 750 BC – 650 BC), Sophocles (c.406 BC), Pindar (517 BC – 438 BC) and Sappho (630 BC – 580 BC) also the Latin poets Virgil (70 BC - 19 BC), Martal (AD 1 – AD 103), and Lucan (AD 39 – AD 65)? Why compare Egil's Saga to these ancient Heathen poets? It is because of the structure of the plot. *Þórólfr Skalla-Grímssonar* is shown as the tragic honest hero and *Egil* as the psycho anti-hero. The Saga narrative is characteristic of Aristotle's analysis, *mimesis* - μιμησιζ, imitation of human behaviour, the other, *katharsis* - καθαρσιζ, emotional cleansing,

> "the emotions generated by tragedy …… are not in fact allowed to remain burdening
> the mind of the audience. They are discharged in the experience of watching (reading)
> tragedy. This emotional 'defecation or purging' leaves the audiences mind after the
> tragedy is over, not loaded with pity and fear, but lightened of them. The effect is
> thus, the opposite of what Plato had supposed."
>
> *(Aristotles Katharsis Theory)*

There is a dichotomy, a distinction between the two brothers which is inherent in their characteristic traits: *Þórólfr* is an idealist and *Egil* a realist but a realist with dark, unsavoury personae, creating a symbolic interaction. It is important to stress these aspects and notice that this narrative does have a parallel in the Greek World: An audacity that firstly, inspired the hero to do the impossible. Secondly, a wild, irresponsible, immature nature, a product of a love of killing and selfishness. While the former was used by *Þórólfr* to control, the combination of both can be seen in *Egil*. The honest Heroic Ideal, the cleansing of *Þórólfr's* Kathartic tragedy gives way to the tyrannical obsessions of *Egil* who acted deliberately from offensive, belligerent and unlawful attributes – the antithesis of Þórólfr's qualities. Þórólfr is seen as 'Superman', *Egil* as 'Wolfman' inheriting much of his father and grandfather's animal, shape-changing cum berserk characteristics.

As well as this similarity to the Heathen Poets in style and structure, *Egil* displays a talent for poetry - skáldic verse. Poetry reveals the life of a culture, it divulges the 'human and real' to posterity but with Egil there is a powerful paradox in his character. Snorri was aware of this strong aspect and used it as a literary device to control the narrative, creating a tangible, seemingly genuine signal to the reader. This aspect was grasped upon by the authors of the latter part of the saga.

Cedric H. Whitman states,

> "Whether or not Old Comedy is a sound historical source for the study of fifth century Athenian society, (*brought forward in time to Egil's Saga*), in Aristophanes hands it is a powerful refractor of that society more truthful, perhaps about the passionate inner drives and aspirations than about the political or economic details more concerned, at its best, with spiritual wholeness, as all true Classic Art is, than with moralizing about parts."
>
> *(1964 "Aristophanes and the Comic Hero" Cambridge, Mass. p14)*

It is this spiritual wholeness, the Heathen supernatural of the Old Heroic ideal, rather than the age of moralistic qualities that Snorri (and the other authors) were living in. Thus, we have a dichotomy in the evidence of the narrative. For the 'Old Greek Ideal' of the hero had outstayed its heathen cultural use, for the new culture of the tenth century, (now depicted in the thirteenth century), heralded the ordered governance of moralistic laws created by Christianity. Dramatic stories had become a tool in the power struggle of political dialogue, these dynamics highlight the differences between societies and the status of skálds against Christianity. These two distinct Plots of Egil's Saga, Heroic and ordered governance demonstrate a shift from semi-drama, a return to the recent past of spectacular heroic entertainment; the traditional structures of life were uprooted and were on the verge of disappearing altogether, Snorri was seeking a participation mystique in the events of a time past. Here Snorri engages the reader in a totality of an apparent life which the new Christian traditions did not offer. It is very easy to embellish history and novelize it. The old Heathen practices, runes, the magic, the gods and Ragnarök (*Fate of the Gods* or *Twilight of the Gods*). Fantasy is a human desire to imagine other worlds and prediction, both were the opposite of the new laws of Christianity. We see examples of this in *Vafþrúðnismál*, *Lokasenna* and *Sigrdrífumál*. It was Georg Philipp Friedrich Freiherr von Hardenberg (aka Novalis) who said, *"The World becomes a dream and the dream becomes a World."*

Thus, poetic tradition can highlight a difference between events about the composition and the contemporary Icelandic society. Comparison between the literary and historical record creates an image of a new culture, a tangible world, superimposed on an old culture. One should not attempt to assume that the image portrayed by tradition is an image of the same society. The events in traditions may not have occurred, or may be embellished, or written by a person other than the original author. This may have happened a few hundred years later for political reasons; these events may have absent people, or certain names may have been positioned as kin of a different family. The authors would therefore, have a vested interest in their skewed narrative.

Also, the narrative may not be contemporary with the events it claims to depict. Thus, to make a comparison between known historical /archaeological data against tradition and written narrative is very important. However, a test for tradition v. written stories may be made against the date of the phrases or words employed from specific cultural values and classifying chronological deployment in Icelandic society. It is this aspect that demonstrates the age of the phrase, indicating a later insertion, a group type, of poems or tales into the narrative.

Noticably, Icelandic Society was in a state of change concerning Heathenism and Christianity. The poems do not explain the loss of Heathenism as a desire to turn the clock back but rather they tell us about the new structures of the present i.e. the time when the saga was written. Archaeology's advantage over history is that it is markedly receptive to the group type of composition. Further, the nature of oral tradition implies that the construction of the narrative may have altered, not just by recall of earlier versions but by repetition. Indeed, the Homeric view of group type/formulae gives way to social phrases - a distinction between linguistic differences amongst Heathenism and Christianity, in Old Scandinavian, Greek and Latin. The inception date of these phrases can provide a correct literary chronological analysis.

The 'Hesiodic' view of Egil's family arguments with authority reveals a disillusioned view of biased justice, through a wrongful partition of an estate, that Egil percieves as his inheritance. It is this constantly recurring argument and the exposeé of the virtues and immoralities represented in a poignant manner which demonstrates a Homeric style. This was a general literary device, a tactic by the author to persuade the reader of Egil's rights introducing an emotional effect but again it was specifically targeted and deployed as a persuasive approach which exploited the situation.

Egil reveals his character, (which does not have highly developed moral, diplomatic and political values), his bullying and threatening behaviour to procure his way by force. He employs divine Heathen intervention – that of Óðinn, who sees all, coupled with the immoral Nið. Yet, if he adopted moral and political values he would probably have achieved more, this illustrates a sub-plot to Egil's character (similar to the formulaeic rhetoric employed by Virgil in the Iliad).

Torfi Túlunius 2002 p32 describes a narrative construction which when applied to Egil's Saga, a thirteenth century story demonstrates a framework that, "conveys a meaning that the teller wants the listener or reader to grasp". This type of framework instills the reader enthusiastically assuming that all narrative is true which it is patiently not and which must be treated with caution. Yet, Egil's Saga has false statements, added phrases and narrative becomes fictional.

Túlunius describes narratology,

> "i) The story, like a description, is a representation, but whereas a description represents something in statis, a story represents an event, the passage from one state to another, or transformation.

ii) The minimal story therefore would be the description of a change in state.

iii) Vladimir Propp's *Morphology of the Folktale* in 1928 was concerned with the concept of function, that is the assessment of characters according to the roles the play in plot development above all else, with less importance given to character traits. This enables a story to be described as an artifact incorporating a certain number of functions strung along a chronological axis.

iv) Certain stages are especially visible in the folktale, though they exist in every story: the stage of exposition, the stage of complication, and the stage of resolution."

These stages are most noticeable in the first twenty-two chapters, after that events are irregularily juxtaposed so that chronological narrative is incorrect. The text highlights contradictions. With these aspects in our minds we illustrate a number of aspects whose veracity is questionable. The curious question of Egil at Brúnanburh, which was a pivotal point in our countries past but the events in Egil's Saga must be treated with caution, as it was collated approximately three centuries after the AD 937 battle[6] took place. This is one aspect against employing Egil's Saga for correct validation of events. With such a delay in narration, implies fictional embellishments may well have transpired, because of the battles importance in establishing the kingdom of England.

Einarsson (2003:185) states, "Considerable parts of the (Egil's) saga appear to be the product of imagination based on earlier literature", also that various 'hands' added to the Saga as well as conflation of different MSS; even in 1894 York Powell had concluded, "Historically dubious with extraneous additions". As such it is unreliable not only because of the late date of compilation, but also on prose stylistic grounds[7]. Interestingly, Slavica Ranović et al (Ed. 2012, 22) employ the phrase the "distributed author" for a collective authorship of Egil's Saga.

The nature of this saga's confused literary state, in part, is clarified by Haukur Þórgeirsson (2014), consisting of two major stylistic features (*ok er – and is* and *en er – but is*) forming an historic palimpsest; thus, indicating that one or more different writers contributed to the saga at a later stage, after Snorri Sturluson who allegedly wrote it c. AD 1240-1. He also wrote the *Edda*[8] and was an historian to the Norwegian Kings, writing *Heimskingla*. As a result, there is every reason to question Egil's Saga as Snorri used his own theories to enhance his status at the Norwegian court[9]. This upset important people, who had their own designs on control in Iceland, with the status of Jarl in the offing; the politics of which created great animosity and were to rebound on Snorri causing his death at his pool. Germaine to the *ok er* and *en er* styles there are a number of devices employed to give credibility, types of structural allusion. This gives credence to the belief that the author or others embellished the saga. There are distinct reasons why he inserts these various structural devices into the narrative to make the reader believe an event later on, because it was alluded to before. Some examples are:

[6.] Egil's Saga was collated approx. 305/6 years after the events therein.
[7.] See Þórgeirsson, 2014, 61-74; who cites Hallberg, 1968, 170.
[8.] "The clearest and most appealing account of (Scandinavian) mythology to modern readers" (Lindow 2001).
[9.] Anderson 2006 "a landed man" becoming the jarl of Iceland under the Norwegian king.

(1) Clunies Ross (2005 rept. 2011. 22) points out that *runhenda* (end rhyme) in the saga was "a change possibly influenced by Norse poets' acquainted with Latin hymns in England or Ireland" as such it is hard indeed to see Egil reading Latin or reciting hymns! Therefore, an argument can be made that this was an 11th century device. Haugen (2002 95.1:824) also points out that, "Several Norwegian bishops during the reign of King *Óláfr Haraldsson* (d. 1030) had learnt to write in England" – this is nearly 100 years after *Eiríkr blóðøx* at York (AD 947-948 and AD 950-954) and *Brúnanburh* (AD 937)!

(2) The provenance of *Höfuðlausn* is crucial; here are further discrepancies: conspicuously if *Höfuðlausn* was composed c. AD 947-948 (which appears unlikely), it would place the poem a decade after *Brúnanburh* and nearly 100 years before this literary device, *runhenda,* was popularly employed. Jónas Kristjánsson (1977, 448-472; 1990, 104) maintains the saga was composed before AD 1250[10] which is probably correct but his possible date of composition between the years AD 1230 and AD 1240 is highly improbable. Notice the continuity of narrative flow in the first twenty-two chapters and then the disjointed nature of events after. Hines (1994-97, 84) indicates stylistically *Höfuðlausn* is employed as a marker 'of time, person and place'. Yet, this cannot be correct as this device was clearly a later structural allusion, for its use implies a chronological dysfunctionality within the narrative questioning whether Egil was in England at the time of Brúnanburh. In addition, Hines (p.83) cites "Sigurður Nordal (who) epitomises a tradition of critical disquiet by summing *Höfuðlausn* up as *'efnislítið og minna listaverk en bezti skáldskapur Egils annar'* (insubstantial, and a lesser work of art than the best of Egil's other work', Nordal 1933, xxi)". Consequently, a date for *Höfuðlausn* must be around AD 1240-46, when it was inserted into the saga to give stylistic credibility. This date was after Snorri had been killed, so neither Egil nor Snorri could have written it.

(3) Noticeable is the title of the poem, *Höfuðlausn* (Head-ransom) "which only appears in medieval prose sources much later than the poem itself" (Clunies Ross 2004, 114-18)[11] such an aspect raises further doubt.

These three aspects above demonstrate literary devices inserted into the narrative. They rely on the author's contemporary scholarship (AD 1220-1240), not the oral traditions three hundred years earlier, for Haugen (2002 95.1: 825) highlights, "The earliest manuscript in the vernacular is AM 655IX 4to, three leaves of an Old Norse translation of Latin legends, which are dated to the second half of the 12th century, possibly as early as AD 1150." [12] Additional writers may have changed the story further by placing the emphasis wholly on Egil, even though other characters were involved. This 'skewing' of the narrative can be demonstrated not only by the later age of the literary devices but also from the historical people involved.

---

[10] Kristjánsson cites Torfi H. Túlunius 2002 *The Matter of the North: the rise of literary fiction in thirteenth-century Iceland.* (trans. Randi C. Eldevik) Odense University Press.

[11] This clearly indicates insertion into the saga, as the *Arinbjarnarkviða,* a praise poem to *Arinbjǫrn Þórisson,* (where the first mention is made of the title) is quoted in *Mǫðruvallabók* (Nordal, Guðrún. 2001 pt 3 p 248: "*Arinbjarnarkviða* is not rendered in Egil's Saga in the saga's manuscripts only one medieval manuscript preserved it at the end of this saga." See AM 132 fol-mid 14th century; also, Anderson 1994) and not found in the saga (Clunies Ross 2005 rept. 2011. 87).

[12] The date is suspect as this was before Snorri was born (AD 1179-1241) if he had written the saga for he was 62 when he was killed, but it may imply there was an original Saga MS and Snorri merged them together to form Egil's Saga. We have no means of knowing the title of this other saga but it could have been about a warrior that fought at Brunanburh.

Jakobsson (2015 p.5) notices that "Snorri relies heavily on his representation in the narrative attributed to his nephew *Sturla Þordarson* (AD 1214-1284), the second best known author of the period."
Karlsson (2002 96.1:832) underlines this fact that noticeably, "Such (Latin) books no doubt existed in Iceland after Christianity was adopted in the year 1000 and in the 11th century with the organization of the Icelandic church."

It was only in the summer of AD 1117-18 that laws and sagas were committed to writing at *Reykjahólar* with *Hafliði Másson* and at this time, or slightly before, Icelanders "had some experience in writing the vernacular in Latin script."[13] Unfortunately for Snorri and the other authors, the use of Latin devices in Iceland clearly emphasizes a later date for *Höfuðlausn* placing it c. AD 1160-1242 (See Tómasson, Sverrir 2002, 91. 793-800). Especially, if another person gathers the information obtained by the original collator – a lack of understanding and verifiable continuity occurs. Byock's explanation seems reasonable (2004: 300-1), "An active process, social memory allows history to be shaped in the image and interests of a community's needs……. stories are altered again and again to meet the needs and expectations of a changing contemporary audience." However, this is in part contrary to her conclusion (p314), "the sagas reinvigorated the actions of ancestors by employing a remembered, rather than invented past." While the telling of sagas' may have culturally reinvigorated later generations, memories handed down over three centuries are altered in the process, the actions of some can actually invent the past! This appears to be the case with Egil's Saga. Oral traditions are valuable only that they illustrate and preserve in the memory, some social and geographical aspects. Nevertheless, when interpreted through careful investigation, comparing historical information with the narrative, a correct verification of the evidence may be obtained even from a negative viewpoint; but *'caveat emptor'* because of their susceptible nature they can be manipulated by others for their (or Snorri's and other editors) purpose, thus skewing the historical accuracy (see Kristinsson 2007). This appears to have happened with Egil's Saga to gain a socio-political advantage. This is recorded in Egil's Saga as many of these traditions, especially *Brúnanburh*, appear to descend from the marriage of *Iófríð Gunnarsdóttir* and *Thorsteinn Egilsson* not from *Egil*, Snorri or the other authors 'skew' this aspect[14] The evidence for this traditional Christian marriage is recorded not only in *Egils, Laxdaela, Kristni* and *Höensa Þórirs Sagas* but also in *Landnámabók*. With so much evidence clearly derived from oral sources, all stating the same facts, it has an element of truth as it is clearly recorded. Snorri cannot exclude or change this evidence for Icelanders would have dismissed Egil's Saga as the quality of his scholarship would be incorrect.

If other writers had assembled Snorri's notes after Snorri's death, then a distinct lack of contextual understanding would be inherent demonstrating their deficiency. This seems to be the case. This writer returns to an astute statement of Todorov (1970) cited by Torfi Túlunius (2000, p527),

> "Genres are an important element in the communication between authors and readers since the generic markers tell the reader into what kind of world he is being led and – in consequence – how he is to interpret the work."

---
[13] See Appendix A – the genealogy of Christian Relationships in Iceland and England.
[14] See Genealogical Evidence Figure 9, p43. This remarkable family tree of the Christian Jarls of Southern Northumbria highlights the unique important relationships to other families in this country and Iceland.

Torfi (2014 Pt.2 Chpt 7 p.294) [15] states, "If Egils Saga founds a genre, it is also a 'highly personal work' as is clear from the way the author sets out to pose riddles". This phrase cannot be acceptable as a piece of individual work as it appears to have been collated by Snorri, and most probably written by Sturla Þordarson his nephew, plus modified by others. One cannot ascribe this saga as the product of one author judging from the structure and the contrasting narrative to historical evidence - there must have been multiple authors. With regard to this last argument Guðrún Nordal (1991-2) in her lecture pointed out that in AD 1230 Sturla definitely contributed to various sagas,

> *"Nú tók at batna með þeim Snorra ok Sturlu, ok var Sturla löngum þá í Reykjaholti ok lagði mikinn hug á at láta rita sögubækr eftir bókum þeim, er Snorri setti saman".*
>
> (Things began to go better between Snorri and Sturla. Sturla spent some considerable time at Reykjaholt, and was very concerned with transcribing books of sagas, from the books that Snorri put together).

Initially, Snorri had his own reasons for fabricating various aspects of the narrative – promoting himself and enhancing his political image. There are 'riddles/kennings in the Saga that may be construed in different ways, some derived from the ancient oral Heroic tradition, others written in the post conversion period of the 13th century.

Torfi suggests that the "authors attempt to *yrkja fólgið* 'compose in a veiled manner'" reveals Christianity. Yet, it masks Snorri's true purpose, as a rival to Sturla for the title Earl of Iceland under the Norweigan Crown - a parapraxis, because he had seriously upset his extended family. Although the saga was probably in collated form, projection was a way for Snorri to publically convey to Sighvatr and Sturla Sighvatsson his contrition for previous conflicts. Both Sighvatr and Sturla were later killed during the *Battle of Örlygsstaðir* (August AD 1238) against *Gizzur Þorvaldsson* and *Kolbein the Young*. In much of Europe during the ninth century, monastic learning seriously declined. Roughton (2009, 2: 816-822) [16] explains the Christian histography, "the structure of the narrative according to the paradigmatic framework to the life of a holy confessor thereby securing its (and its subjects) cultural legitimacy. This framework well known in hagiography emphasizes its subject's excellence as an *imitatio Christi*". Yet, if we compare this to the Saga, Egil's characteristics and traits are in fact the reverse of Christian holiness and emphasize Heathenism - Egil's unvirtuous *Óðinnic* idiosyncrasies. It is almost as if the author(s) - it is worth stressing this duality, are creating a diametrically opposed version of *Óðinnic* hagiography to that of Christian hagiography. Yet, it was collated and written in Christian times from, in some cases old oral traditions; the question is, 'where did these belief's come from?' as they appear to be from other sagas, even possibly other events.

---

[15] Túlunius, Torfi H. 2014 *The Enigma of Egil: The Saga, the Viking Poet and Snorri Sturluson.* Islandica Vol. LVII translated by Victoria Cribb. Ed. P.J. Stevens. Cornell University Library, Ithaca, New York.

[16] Roughton, Philip. 2009 *A Hagiographical Reading of Egils Saga.* The 14th International Saga Conference, Uppsala 9th-15th August 2009. Vol. 2. In *Á austrvega – Saga and East Scandinavia*. Eds. Agneta Ney, Henrik Williams and Fredrik Charpentier Ljungqvist in cooperation with Marco Bianchi, Maja Bäckvall, Lennart Elmevik, Anne-Sofie Gräslund, Heimir Pálsson, Lasse Mårtensson, Olof Sundqvist, Daniel Sävborg and Per Vikstrand. Papers from the Dept of Humanities and Social Sciences 14. Institute for Language and Folklore, University of Gävle: Gävle University Press. 2009:816-822.

Predominantly, there are two divergent themes as the saga first expresses Heathenism and is then tempered with elements of Christianity, but it is Egil's love of Heathenism that emanates strongly and places him firmly in the heathen 'camp'.

This short analysis demonstrates that Egil's Saga appears to be a concoction of different philosophies and phrases from different time periods forming a palimpsest from what seems to be two or more different sagas and traditions. When these time periods are analyzed interesting historical aspects occur that show chronological mismatches. Therefore, from a literary angle with so many discrepancies in its construction we must consider much of the historical evidence in the saga as dubious.

Tulinius (2014:34) states that the first part of Egil's Saga, the tale of *Þórólfr Kveld-Ulfsson,* has a coherence of narrative and may have been composed by Snorri but "the second part spans some 90 years and seems somewhat disjointed".

Anderson (1967:107) asserts "that it fails to display the same command of his materials." This section appears as a 'bolt on' part to the tragedy of *Þórólfr*. It is noticeable that Snorri may only have had time to think and construct the first part of the saga i.e. chapters 1 to 22 between the years AD 1237-39 for Snorri was in Norway staying with *earl Skúli*. He returns to Iceland in spite of *King Hákon's* ban. The next two years may have given some substance to the first part of the story. How much was collated from Snorri's notes and how much was introduced into the second part of the saga we may never know the full story.

It is the disjointed sections of the second part that highlight extracts and influences - they have become preserved and altered in the 'memory' of this saga. The time and space between these sections 'exhibit qualities of artistic design usually associated with individual authorship'.

If other writers had assembled Snorri's notes after his death, then a distinct lack of contextual understanding would be inherent demonstrating their deficiency. This seems to be the case. Anderson (1967:21-22) argues that, 'the second part of the saga lacks coherence'. Stylistically, the first part of the saga up to the twenty-second chapter Anderson states, 'No element is extraneous each is carefully placed to create maximum effect.'

With this in mind the argument that *Sturla Þórðarson* may have written this saga seems to gather validity; *Sturla* would have been 26 years old at the time of Snorri's death and would be gathering the knowledge of authorship. It should be noted that *Sturla* wrote *Hákonar saga Hákonarsonar* c. AD 1265 when he was 51 and *Íslandinga saga* c. AD 1280 when he was 66. These two sagas are attributed to *Sturla* as the author from contemporary accounts. It is a notable fact that the oldest manuscript the theta fragment (AM 162 A Θ fol.), dated to c. AD 1250 places this manuscript at the time of *Sturla*. Tulinius proposes three assumptions:

i) Much that was previously believed to be based on such an oral tradition is actually borrowed more or less openly from other works of literature, autochthronous or foreign. (Tulinius 2013 cites Einarsson 1975; Hafstad 1995).

ii) An assumption is that Egil's Saga is the earliest of the *Íslendingasogur* or saga about early Icelanders and it is the founding saga of a genre...... if it is not the progenitor of the genre it is quite likely its first great text and it can therefore be said to have consolidated the genre.

iii) The saga is older than its earliest manuscript fragment dated to AD 1250. Nor does anybody doubt that the saga was completed by someone in Snorri's milieu.

In answer to these above three issues they raise the questions that,

a) The closeness of Gunnar's Stead at *Örnolfsdal* to *Reykjaholt* with Snorri coupled with *Iófríð's* marrage to *Thorstein Egilsson* and the status of *Gunnar* means a Saga was probably written about him.

b) This lost Saga would have formed the basis of Egil's Saga and therefore, was originally the start of the genre. Snorri would have wanted to have placed Egil Saga as the foremost of the genre which would be in keeping with his inflated politics to project his image as the Jarl of Iceland. Demonstrably, there must have been an original Hesiodic style family saga.

c) Interestingly other scholars and authorities confirm that most of Egils Saga was not written by Snorri. This corroborates the view that the first twenty-two chapters of Egils Saga were probably written by Snorri and the rest of the chapters were written by one or more different people drawing on lost sources especially about Brúnanburh.

In the latter part of the Saga (those chapters from twenty-two to the end), these chapters show no real narrative flow. They are unpredictable and erratic with aspects and poems inserted at a later stage. As such we should seriously enquire, analyse and compare the content to historical data, they should be placed under close scrutiny. Certainly, when compared to the historical timeline of Gunnar's life, his status and events, there is a quite remarkable closeness. So remarkably close that it cannot be mere coincidence.

PAGAN RITUAL CONTRASTED TO EARLY CHRISTIAN BELIEFS

Poets were called skálds cultivating a priest status; use of the umlaut in Scandinavian language created three cultural orders: legal, religious and social, forming a balanced cohesion. Linguistically, they created tonal sounds within a group of lines forming rhyme to a lyric poem. These cultural linguistic orders also controlled the behaviour of the people. *Bragi the Old, Jarl Törf Einar Rognvaldsson,* belonged to an early style of skáldship highlighting archaic fronted assonance in the strophes and assonance across lines, which look random but are controlled by various sounds and probably ritually sung; *Jarl Gunnar Þórrøðrsson* (aka *Hlífrsson*), *Egil Skallagrímsson,* belonged to the cusp of change into the Post Christian period with a few archaic but mainly developed assonance, employing sounds creating meaning and using obtuse kennings. Skálds were complying with rigorous metrical laws when composing verse and illustrated heathen myth and legend as graphic imagery, including 'kennings' of specific meaning (a type of trope – a rhetorical figure of speech that combined two different aspects into one, a play on words).

The utilization of 'riddle types' of word were held in high esteem, for they were capable of immortalizing or vilifying high born or common people. The spoken language (*dönsk tunga*) was interwoven with meaning becoming 'monumental' especially when engraved on stone.

In Anglo-Saxon culture, a hermeneutic style regenerating Christianity was prevalent circa AD 973 (i.e. the *Regularis Concordia* written by *Æthelwold* at Winchester) and this style influenced the beliefs of Northern England at that time. Interestingly, the style was not prevalent in Iceland. *Orm Barryjaskáld* preceded *Snorri* and was influenced by neo-archaic assonance (referring back to ancient Greek poetry) coupled with end rhyme and Christian 'images'; all were able to compose with the spoken word and with runes. As this 'end rhyme' occurred chronologically late, we must ascribe *Egil's* verses to *Snorri* or the other authors and clearly **not** to *Egil* (See page 11, 1). As previously mentioned, 'umlaut structure' within the language created three meanings to one word: general usage/legal/religious. Guthmundson (1967)[17] maintains that there was every reason to believe that skálds played a much greater role in the heathen religion than is realized, their understanding of praise and ridicule had political as well as religious significance. Constructing untrue verses about one or being economical with, or twisting information, amounted to a defamatory and malicious slander, also engraving them on stone or writing them on paper could easily result in vilification, a libel. All were abhorrent to the Church. As a result of Christianity, skáldship became a poetic channel of compliments and emotion rather than one of premeditated ritual character assassination employing spirit possession and sorcery.

Historical sources emphasize that as the Scandinavians pushed further west they came into contact with the Christian world. Ireland and the petty kingdoms of Wessex, Mercia, East Anglia and Northumbria were nations that fostered the spread of Christianity against Heathenism; from these kingdom's the Carolingian empire sought its church leaders. There are poems that show traces of an early transition between Heathenism and Christian influence such as *Skírnismál* (Codex Regius GKS 2365 4to) that highlight the influence of the Salic Law. Dating *Skírnismáls* influence: Gunnell (1995)[18] regards Bertha Phillpotts' work (1920)[19] as the 'high water mark' identifying *Skírnismál* as a performance drama. Further, Gunnell cites Guðbrandur Vígfússon and F. York-Powell (1883) who stated that because of its dialogic form *Skírnismál* may have been composed in the Western Islands. Dronke (1997)[20] reinforces this view and is of the opinion that "the style of *Skírnismál* was professionally out-of-date for court poets of the late tenth century, thus indicating a ninth century composition date."

The datable style of *Skírnismál's* dialogic form corresponds to AD 830-860, exactly the date we are concerned with for an early Scandinavian kingdom in southern Cumbria and its links with the Christian Anglian Northumbrian kingdom which we shall discuss later. Christian thinking was reintroduced to the Carolingian Empire from the learned scholars of the west in the form of Homilies.

---

[17] Guthmundson, Barthi (1967) Barthi had a great depth of knowledge on this subject and traced it back to the Heurli tribe during the migration age who he believed brought runic writing to the north.

[18] Gunnell, Terry 1995 *The Origins of Drama in Scandinavian.* D.S. Brewer – Boydell & Brewer.

[19] Phillpotts, Bertha S., 1920 *The Elder Edda and ancient Scandinavian drama.* Cambridge.

[20] Dronke, Peter (1979) *A note on Pamphilus.* The Journal of the Warburg and Courthauld Institutes. 42, 225-230; see also Dronke 1991 *Latin and vernacular poets of the Middle Ages.* Aldershot.

The MS St Gallen, Stiftsbibliothek, Codex Sang. 558 dated from AD 922 – 926 is a series of chants. Even earlier (circa 6th century) St Martin of Braga's *"De correctione rusticorum"* was employed by missionaries to impart the Christian faith to check paganism. This was used by Charlemagne for the advantage of the Church and this great Capitulary underlies an accurate appreciation of the scriptures; both the *Admonitio generalis,* and his *De litteris colendis* (Chazelle & Edwards 2003)[21] demonstrate to laity and clergy the importance of the Word as a means of instilling Christianity into the heathen. During the Carolingian period, Biblical exegesis was the principal mode of Christian erudition for the missionaries.

A classic example of Christian law is cited by Torfi (2014 Pt.1, Chpt 2, p66) who points out Egil's anxiety over *Ásgerðr*," It was a universal rule in medieval canon law that a man was forbidden to marry his brother's widow. A clause from the *Grágás* (– the Early Laws of Iceland), shows this ban was in effect in Iceland at the time Egil's Saga was written".

Heathenism's opposing word is found in *Kristni Saga* (Vigfússon and Powell Vol.2, 1905[22]; see p.37 Genealogical analysis: *Jarl Gunnar Hlífrsson's family relationship with Thorsteinn Egilsson* and Appendix A of this article) plus *Gizzur the White* and *Hjalti* and the Bible translation after the conversion to Christianity c. AD 1000. Other later secular influences were *Fyrsta Málfrædiritgerdin* (The First Grammatical Treatise). It is the first of four books found in the *Codex Wormianus* (AM 242 fol.). Written in Old Norse it is dated to AD 1125-1175 during the true linguistic period of Old Norse. This was just after the 'conference of scholars', "In the winter of AD 1117-18 the secular laws were revised and written down … at the farm of *Haflidi Masson*" (Sørensen 1993 p 52)[23] possibly by Ingmundr the Priest who had been trained in England. (see Appendix A of this article). It seems Sagas were discussed in the winter of AD 1118-9. However, Guðrún Nordal (2001 p6)[24] states the philosophy was still based on,

> "Classical pagan poets, such as Virgil, Horace and Ovid were the great authorties in the Latin textual culture which served as the foundation for the emerging vernacular literary culture in Iceland in the eleventh century."

As we have seen other Classical pagan poets (the Greeks, Homer and Hesiod), their influence was considerable and their philosophy may be found in various sagas. After a period (AD 826 to AD 850) in the early medieval era, the resurgence of Heathenism in the west and the isolation of Iceland caused some social problems as quarrels and disputes found in the sagas testify.

---

[21] Chazelle, Celia & Edwards, Burton v. N. (2003) *The Study of the Bible in the Carolingian Era.* (Medieval Church Studies 3), Turnhout, Brepolis.

[22] Vígfússon, Gudbrand & York-Powell, F. 1905 *Origines Islandicae* Vol.2, Oxford.

[23] Sørensen, Preben Meulengracht.1993 *Saga and society: an introduction to Old Norse literature.* Trans. John Tucker. (Studia Borealia/Norse Studies, Monograph Series I). Odense: Odense Univ. Press.

[24] Guðrún Nordal 2001 *Skaldic Versifying and Social Discrimination in Medieval Iceland.* The Dorothea Memorial Lecture. (15 March 2001). Viking Society for Northern Research. UCL.

HISTORICAL AND ARCHAEOLOGICAL EVIDENCE

Historical chronology. While there is no doubt that Egil was a great warrior, his presence at *Brúnanburh* for *Æthelstan* was extremely doubtful. For example, Snorri, plus the later collective authorship of Egil's Saga, besmirches the Northumbrian Jarls of Amounderness i.e. Southern Northumbria, who were Danish and eliminates not just them but all Danes from Egil's story. This highlights a slant towards a Norwegian viewpoint.

Yet, historically, in AD 934, three years before the Battle of *Brúnanburh*, *Æthelstan* had gathered his forces at Nottingham for an invasion of Scotland. His strategy was clear, to re-establish Christian Northumbria, stop Heathenism but his immediate concern was the Scots and Strathclyde Welsh intriguing with the Heathen Hiberno-Norse of Dublin.[24] Previously *Æthelstan* had purchased the area of Amounderness from a Heathen and had issued a Charter at Nottingham,[25] donating this area to Archbishop *Wulfstan I* of St Peter's, York. One of the witnesses to this Charter, Anglo Danish: *Jarl Þurferd* / O.N.: *Þórrøðr* was the Christian Jarl of Northampton who was given charge of Amounderness for the church at York[26].

Such confidence demonstrates that many Danes of the Danelaw were devout Christians. Seventeen years before, this Christian jarl of the Danelaw, *Jarl Þurferd*, had submitted to *Æthelstan's* father *Edward the Elder* (AD 917 ASaxChron), had taken an oath to support him and had remained loyal.

Unfortunately, *Jarl Þurferd / Þórrøðr* was killed in battle on *Æthelstan's* Scottish invasion later in that year (AD 934) and his son *Jarl Gunnar* inherited the jarldom. It should be noted the Anglo Danish: *Jarl Þurferd* had married *Hlifr* the daughter of *Törf Einar Rognvaldsson*, hence the linguistic change to O.N.: *Þórrøðr*. As the hereditary Christian Jarl of Amounderness, *Gunnar* fought for *Æthelstan* at the Battle of *Brúnanburh* as one of his captains and survived, standing alongside his friend *King Æthelstan*, leading the Christian contingent of the Danelaw into the battle, thus forming the Nation State of England. His status, courage and ability are clearly recognised in *Höensa-Þóris Saga*[27], *Laxdaela Saga*[28] and *Landnámabók*[29] which Snorri and others choose to ignore. It is not clear but the Jarldom of Amounderness may well have included Furness, as the home estate of Anglo Danish: *Jarl Þurferd* / O.N. *Jarl Þórrøðr* was on Furness. Both were part of the kingdom of Northumbria. There are nine pieces of archaeological evidence to support this view:

(i) Low Furness Tithe Maps illustrate very early OE field-names dating from AD 600 to AD 1066. The Common Scandinavian names are very early some dating from AD 830. Field (1972 p.xiii) states, "whether field-names are of proven antiquity or of post-enclosure origin, it will be found that the method of designating plots of land remains essentially the same now as it was in the (Early) Middle Ages".

[25.] Slave trading was the *modus operandi* of the Hiberno-Norse which was an anathema to *Æthelstan* (Wyatt 2009: 30).

[26.] See Sawyer 1968 - S407 ff. 42r-43r AD 930 for AD 934 Nottingham 7th June s.xvii. Importantly see Whitelock, D. (ed.) 1955 *English Historical Documents 1, c. AD 500-1042*. London. No. 104, in answer that this charter was spurious.

[27.] The boundary clauses are specific "West by the sea, north by the river Cocker east by the river Hodder below Dunsop Bridge and south by the river Ribble." E.Y.C. No.1 E.H.D. 1 pp505-8.

[27.] *Höensa-Þóris Saga* (see Morris, W. & Magnusson, E. 1903),

[28.] *Laxdaela Saga* (see Einar Ól Sveinsson 1934)

[29.] *Landnámabók* (see Vígfússon, Guthbrand & York-Powell, F. 1905).

(ii) The stream called the Yarl rises near to *Gerleuuorde* (DB) – jarl's estate, later known as Crosshouse, later still Kirkby Hall at Kirkby-Ireleth.

(iii) Status field-names identify an estate in Low Furness of some importance. This estate was pre-Tostig's manor of Hougun probably occurring between AD 934 -AD 1000. The 1842 Tithe Map (Kew, National Archives 2013) reveals specific field-names [F-N] especially in Dalton Parish – A248/A249 Back Yarl's Field, A276 Yarl's Well Field, A274 Yarl's Well, A275 Yarls Wall, A225 Great Yarl's Field, and A256 Miller Yarl's Field plus the river that rises near Kirkby Hall is known as the Yarl.[30]

(iv) Tostig's land grab must have occurred c. AD 1063-4 this would give him very little time to establish himself within the field-names of the Hougun estate. Thus, indication of the existence of these field-names was permanent before the land grab, i.e. the estate belonged to *Ulfr Dólgfinnsson* (the *Ailward* - the other ward)[31] and his kin were *Gospatric Uchtredson* (the *ward*) and *Gamel Ormson*. *Gospatric* and *Ulfr* were step brothers by their mother *Sige* marring twice, hence their descriptive names *Ailward* and *Ward*. [*The correct explanation of Ailward is derived from OIrish: Ail - the other and Brythonic: Gward, Ward*]. *Ulfr Dólgfinnsson* was the direct descendant of TORHTRED (ON: *Þórrøðr*, ODan: *Þurferth*).

(v) The Urswick Cross Shaft previously dated as early Northumbrian (Bailey & Cramp (1988), was recut with the name TORHTRED (ON: *Þórrøðr*, ODan: *Þurferth*) c. AD 934/6[32].

(vi) R.I. Page (1959 p.402)[33] reads the inscription as *+tunwini setæ æfter toro3tredæ bekun æfter his bæurne gebidæs per saulæ+*. This shaft stood in front of Kirkby Hall, previously known as Crosshouse, originally *Gerleuuorde*, the plinth for the cross can be seen today.

(vii) As early as 1927 Collingwood[34] translates this runic as "*Tunwini set after Torhtred a monument to his lord. Pray for his soul*". Indicating that *Torhtred* (*Þórrøðr*) was Christian.

(viii) *Torhtred* is derived from Common Scandinavian *Þurrauðr*, OWS: *Þórrøðr*, Anglo-Danish: *Thurferth / Þurferð*, shortened to *Thored*, ON: *Þórðr*[35].

---

[30] Kirby, J.R. 2013 *Early Settlements and their related vills on the Furness Peninsula: Dalton Parish c. AD 800-1200*. Unpublished Post-Graduate Dissertation, Dept. of Continuing Education, Oxford University, p27. As these field-names existed before Tostig's 'land grab' because of their early nature, they clearly demonstrate that they belonged to either *Jarl Þurferd* or his son *Jarl Gunnar Þórrøðr* or his son *Jarl Þórrøðr Gunnarson*. Without doubt, this estate was pre-Tostig.

[31] The definition of *Ailward* has been a source of dispute but the author corrects other variations as it is always known in his family as '*the other ward*' and is derived from O. Irish: *Ail - other* and Brythonic: *Gwlad - ward*. The *ward* was *Gospatric Uchtredsson*, *Ulf Dólgfinnsson's* step brother by his mother Sige, daughter of Styr son of Ulfr.

[32] Personal discussion in 2001 between the late R.I. Page, M. Barnes and the author in Senior Common Room at UCL.

[33] R.I. Page (1959) p402.

[34] Collingwood, W. G. 1927 p54. Collingwood did much valuable runic translation work.

[35] von Feilitzen, Otto 1937 The Pre-Conquest Personal Names of Domesday Book (Arkiv for Germans Namnforskning Utgivet AV Joran Sahlgren).

(ix) As *Þórrøðr* was a *Jarl* in Furness at the same time as *Jarl Þórrøðr* was placed in charge of Amounderness, answerable to *Archbishop Wulfstan I of York* who was his overlord, we must conclude they are one and the same. There is no one of that status at that time in that area with that name. *Æthelstan* gave Amounderness to *Wulstan I* in the Nottingham Charter of AD 934. *Þórrøðr* was one of the witnesses to this Charter[36]. He was previously Jarl of Northampton under *Edward the Elder* to whom he submitted, took an oath of fealty and kept his Jarldom in AD 917.

(x) Kirkby-Ireleth Church was known as one of the resting places for the relics of St Cuthbert being the furthest west of the Northumbrian kingdom.

(xi) The Urswick family had intermarried with the Kirkby family c. AD 1480. (Bodleian Library Dodsworth MSS 5. f.123). Both families were neighbours on the Furness peninsula.

Figure 1. The Urswick Sculpture. Raymond Page (1959, 144) suggested a date of 'between AD 750 and AD 850' for the original inscription on the cross. However, he states, the recutting of *Torhtred* is datable to AD 934/5, a date just after *Þórrøðr* was killed in battle. This shard of the cross originally stood in front of Kirkby Hall (© J.R. Kirby 2015).

Figure 2. Kirkby Hall known as Crosshouse – the plinth of the cross can still be seen in front of the gate. This manor was originally known as *Gerleuuorde* (DB) the jarl's estate (after *Þórrøðr*). (© J.R. Kirby 2002).

[36.] Sawyer. P.H. 1968 *Anglo-Saxon Charters. An Annotated List and Bibliography.* Royal Historical Society Guides and Handbooks, 8 London No.520. See Charter S407 at Nottingham in AD 934. (See S416 & S425 for more names of the Jarls of the Danelaw).

THE SOCIO-RELIGIOUS SPHERE

Religion: Christianity v. Heathenism. *Jarl Gunnar Þórrøðrsson* travelled to Iceland before *Æthelstan's* death c.AD 940, (he returned to England *c.* AD 950-952 with his eldest son). When in Iceland he took his matronymic name *Hlífrsson*, because of his association with *Æthelstan* and Christianity. *Hlífr* was the daughter of *Jarl Törf Einar Rognvaldsson* (who was a notable skáld) and the Christian *Queen Þurriðr* the widow of *King Þursteinn Rauðr* (*Landnámabók*) [37]. Barthi Guthmundsson (1967) notes clearly the use of a matronymic was employed by skálds[38]. Poetry was retained when the Heathen religion was dropped. This change of name may also have had a double use to disguise his real identity - *Gunnar Þórrøðrsson* (aka *Hlífrsson*) or to show his family status.

The Icelandic settlement (*Landnáma*) might have continued longer than thought for Smith (1995) advocates' "archaeological analysis highlights a longer period of settlement possibly around a century rather than AD 870-930" [39]. While out in Iceland, *Gunnar's* jarldom of Amounderness was re-attacked by the opposing forces. In Iceland, he married *Helga*, the daughter of *Alfdís of Barra* and *Prince Óláfr Fealán* [40], the son of *King Þursteinnr inn Rauðr*, who was an early king of southern Cumbria and western Northumbria *c.* AD 850-865. Coniston Water was named after him, for before 1785 it was called *Þursteinnr's Flu*. Collingwood (1895) wrote a semi-fictional story[41] about the historical *King Þursteinnr* who was a Christian against the wishes of his father, the Heathen *King Óláfr inn Hviti*.

Figure 3. Furness Peninsula circa 1570-90 (British Library, map of Furness peninsula. No 83326). Notice the original name for Coniston Water was Thursteinn's Flu.

---

[37] *Landnámabók* Vígfússon, Guthbrand & York-Powell, F. 1905.*Origines Islandicae* Vol 1. Oxford.
[38] Barthi Guthmundsson 1967 *The Origin of the Icelanders*. Trans. & intro by Lee Hollander. University of Nebraska Press.
[39] Smith, Kevin P. 1995 "Landnám. The settlement of Iceland in archaeological and historical perspective." World Archaeology 26/3: 319-47.
[40] *Helga*, the daughter of *Alfdís of Barra* and *Óláfr Fealán* of Hvamm in the western dales of Iceland. (*Landnámabók*).
[41] Collingwood, William Gershom 1895 *Thorstein of the Mere. A Saga of the Northmen in Lakeland*. London: Edward Arnold.

This semi-fictional story was perceived as changing reality to fiction rather than a type of saga, which was unfortunate. Even to this day the area south of Coniston is known as Thorstein's Vale. The link here is that *Alfdís of Barra* was born in Furness; *Gunnar* and *Helga* had four children: *Rauðr (Þórrøðr)*, *Vrai* who was nicknamed *Höggvandil* (after Gunnar's ring-sword), *Þurríðr (Höensa Thorirs and Brennu Njalls Saga,)* and *Iófríð* (*Egil's Saga, Höensa Thorirs Saga, Gunnlaugr Ormstunga Saga and Laxdaela Saga*; see *Landnámabók* 1905, II.15.7-11, Bk 1, 84; see page 44 - *Genealogical Analysis* of this article; see also Appendix A - *Christian Relationships in Iceland and England*. P50). Gunnar's Christian background is emphasized by his sister *Þórgerd* who married *Skeggi*, for she had travelled to Iceland with him. Their son was *Hjalti* who married *Vibjorg* daughter of *Gizzur inn Hviti* – both *Hjalti* and *Gizzur* brought Christianity to Iceland c. AD 1000, (*Kristni Saga*). They had formed not only family relationships but trading ports between Iceland, Norway and North-West England. Even earlier than *Gizzur*[42] and *Hjalti* pursuing Christianity was *Queen Aud the Deepminded* whose landtake was around Hvammsfjorðr, Dalasýsla. The Christian marriage of *Gunnar* to *Helga* was in keeping with traditions of both *Prince Óláfr Fealán* and *Jarl Gunnar's* families but not *Egils*. *Iofríð Gunnarsdóttir* married and converted *Thorstein Egilsson* to Christianity. *Iófríð* and *Thorstein* were given a dowry, 'heinan fylia', (Foote and Wilson 1970 p113) of two chests of coins minted for Æthelstan. However, the important point was it was not *Egil's* money as the saga implies but *Thorstein's*. (See Jacobsen 1978 p37). *Thorstein* administered *Iófríð's* dowry which represented her portion of *Gunnar's* inheritance. [The Saga's chronology is incorrect for it suggests, *"He brings home two chests full of silver, compensation for Þórólfr from the English King Æthelstan, which he is supposed to present to Skallagrímr as a wergild for his son, while part is to be shared among those kinsmen of Þórólfr whom Egil judges most deserving. He himself is to receive compensation for his brother in the form of land or wealth when he returns to the king's court"*. But after his homecoming, the saga states: *"Egil had an enormous amount of wealth, but it is not mentioned whether he ever shared the silver that King Æthelstan had presented to him, either with Skallagrímr or anyone else"*]. There was a distinct reason why Snorri or other writers insert this stratagem - to falsify the narrative, to return later to create a structural allusion in the story: *Egil* threw the money into a marsh, because he was angry with his son *Thorstein* marrying a Christian, whereas his other son *Bodvar* was a Heathen agreeing with *Egil's* religion. This type of behaviour from *Egil* was 'true to form' as *Egil* was avaricious - importantly, *Egil* would **not** have thrown his own money away, (supposedly received from Æthelstan), into the marsh! Therefore, we can seriously question whether *Egil* actually fought at the battle of *Brúnanburh*. This is but one example of doubtful chronology inherent in Egil's Saga. Conversely, these chests act as a dowry for *Thorstein*. The author of Egil's Saga cannot escape this Christian ceremonial fact.

Family relationships show further anomalies, *Bodvar* was drowned and accorded a long emotional testimony, but astonishingly we are not told about another son, *Gunnar*! (Aðalsteinsson 1999 *"the saga supplies no evidence for the existence of a third son"*[43] i.e. *Gunnar*). It has been suggested that the reference in verse 20 of *Sonatorrek* implies *Gunnar* died of a fever but there is no mention of *Gunnar* in the Saga. Significantly, the death of *Egil's* son, *Bodvar*, was accorded a great deal of angst (*Sonatorrek* becomes Egil's 'cry to *Óðinn*')[44] but no such sorrow was given to the death of *Gunnar*, *Egil's* (supposed) other son (see - Genealogical analysis p37).

[42.] *Kristni Saga* Vígfússon, Guthbrand & York-Powell, F. 1916 *Conversion and Early Church in Iceland* Bk 3 Oxford. See also Sián Grønlie (trans.) 2006 *Kristni Saga - The Story of the Conversion* Vol.XVIII Gen.Eds Anthony Fawlkes & Alison Finlay Viking Soc. For Northern Research Text Series. U.C.L.

[43.] Aðalsteinsson 1999 this is a highly important piece of evidence. The omission of Gunnar demonstrates that two sagas have been combined in order to form Egil's Saga.

[44.] *Sonatorrek - this may have been inserted by Sturla Þordarson as the name Gunnar does not run in Egil's family.*

This is out of character, the inclusion of *Gunnar* appears in the later *Sonatorrek*, than the Saga. The name, *Gunnar*, which was *Thorsteinn Egilsson's* father-in-law appears to have been included. *Bodvar* adhered to Heathenism, whereas *Thorsteinn* his brother had adopted Christianity - society was changing and *Thorsteinn* changed with it; the Old Heroic Age to an orderly governed society. Therefore, there are serious concerns about the validity of this *Gunnar Egilsson* especially if we note Aðalsteinsson's statement. Geographically, in Iceland *Gunnar Þórrøðrsson* (aka *Hlífrsson*) had moved from *Gunnarstaðir* (GPS *Gunnarstaðir* N65° 0′ 54.2023″, W21° 56′ 30.3259″) on the *Strand* of *Hvammsfjorðr* to *Örnolfsdalur* (GPS *Örnolfsdalur* N64° 40′ 45.7087″ W21° 27′ 42.4512″) which was across the valley of the *Hvitá* river from *Reykjaholt* Snorri's home (GPS *Reykjaholt*: N64° 39′ 53.661″ W21° 17′ 32.068″); the nearness of these two settlements may have given Snorri and the other editors ideas. Significantly, *Gunnar Hlífrsson* was a skáld who had inherited this love for poetry from *Alfdís of Barra* and *Hlífr* (his mother), *Törf Einar Rognvaldsson's* daughter (for skáldic tradition from the mother see Barthi Guthmundsson, 1967). *Gunnar's* eldest son, was called *Rauðr/ Þórrøðr,* traditionally named after his grandfather, who had been killed in battle (AD 934) before he was born (this tradition is mentioned by Barthi Guthmundsson, 1967; see also Sørensen, Preben Meulengracht. 1993)[45]. *Þórrøðr Gunnarson* is stated as wasting Westmorland in AD 966 (A.S.Chron.), therefore the Anglo-Saxon Crown was thus returning that area back under the control of the church of York and *Þórrøðr's* family. Noticeably, *Gunnar Þorrøðrsson* as the Jarl of Amounderness was influential in the Danelaw because his father was originally Jarl of Northampton. This begs the question, "Was Amounderness in Southern Northumbria regarded as a borough of the Danelaw?" (See page 16 for background). If so it would be another political argument for the invasion by the Pagan Norse. Further, as *Gunnar* had 'jarl' status he was regarded as a captain, unlike *Egil* who was the son of a 'hersir' but had not been given the title.

In all dealings with religion and the supernatural *Egil* chooses the Heathen camp and does not espouse Christian beliefs - there is no conscious tussle of morals in the narrative (Faraday 1906)[46]. Such Christian elements come from *Iofríð Gunnarsdóttir* married to *Thorstein Egilsson* and were interspersed by later Christian constructions to the saga. However, if this evidence is untrustworthy, the questions to be asked are, "Where did these traditions come from?" "Why was *Egil* fighting for a Christian King when he was clearly an Ultra Heathen?" "Would *Æthelstan* have even allowed him into his court let alone his army?"

The answers are startling and demonstrate the story of Egil's Saga was initially concocted and collated by Snorri, (k. 23Sept 1241) but probably written by one of his nephews, the brothers *Þórðarson: Óláf White-Poet* (AD 1210-1259) and *Saga-Sturla* (AD 1214-1284). It was most probably *Saga-Sturla* who also wrote *Íslendinga saga, Sturlunga saga, Kristni Saga* and *Hákonar saga Hákonarsonar* in the 1260's). They were opposed to *Gizzur Þórvaldsson* (d.1268). Each of these characters had their own interest, thus intrigue by Snorri turned into acrimony and then to murder (Jakobsson Ármann 2015)[47]. This article has already demonstrated the Christian argument but can highlight further examples. Rather than Christianity, Heathenism 'screams out' from the written narrative of Egil's Saga for the saga seems to delight in it - an interesting point as it was constructed during Christian times.

---

[45] Guthmundsson, Barthi 1967: *The Origin of the Icelanders.* Trans. & intro by Lee Hollander. University of Nebraska Press; see also Sørensen, Preben Meulengracht.1993 *Saga and society: an introduction to Old Norse literature.* Trans. John Tucker. (Studia Borealia/Norse Studies, Monograph Series I). Odense: Odense Univ. Press.

[46] Faraday 1906: 387-426. Faradays analysis is clearly laid out highlighting Egils ultra-heathen stance.

[47] Jakobsson Ármann 2015 Saga-Book of the Viking Society for Northern Research Vol. XXXIX

Byock (1986, 161) [48] states, *"Egil himself ascribes his poetic genius to Óðinn"* he constantly refers to *Óðinn*, notice the *Höfuðlausn* (Head ransom) poem to *Eiríkr blóðøx* at York ascribed to *Egil* but was probably written by another hand for interestingly it is written in *runhenda* (see page 11 of this article; also, Einarsson, Stefán 1954, 1967) [49]; also, *Óðinn* is found in *Sonartorrek* and *Arinbjarnarkviða; Egil's* verse of *Berg-Onund* etc. *Egil's* religion is clearly Heathen (Hoffman 2007) [50]. The influence of *'runhenda'* demonstrates a later 11th century style. Clunies-Ross (2005, 32) [51] points out that *Höfuðlausn* was not the only head ransom poem - *Óttar Svarti* and *Þórarínn loftunga* were two 11th century poets who employ this device. This implication means the authors of Egil's Saga were imprinting their version of Heathenism on the narrative.

This author turns to the opposing paranormal style expressed in the narrative to impress the point - the religious, supernatural and social status mentioned by Torfi Túlunius employing his framework. The supernatural prevails as *Egil's 'modus operandi'*, his behaviour is 'head-on' and is thus reflected in his lifestyle, the narrative demonstrates his psychopathic mood swings that according to the author were similar to his father and grandfather (*Kveld-Úlf* – Evening Wolf) shape-changers. The burial of his father *Skallagrímr* has all the hallmarks of a Heathen burial, its superstitions, beliefs (Clunies Ross 1989) [52]. Also, it is the loss of social status that is conspicuous in *Egil's* ideology, the jarl status held by his brother *Þórulf* who had gained a higher status than his father, who was a hersir, a landholder of great authority, a driving force in *Egil's* psyche.

This coupled with the loss of his skáldic 'licence', his empowerment amongst his fellows 'spirit world' - the most treasured of Heathen beliefs that hurts *Egil's* soul, being reduced further by Christian beliefs. It is this that causes *Egil* great angst and bitterness. (Margaret Clunies Ross 2005 rept. 2011. 94).

The 'dark spirit world' inherent in *Egil's* Heathen psyche is demonstrated by the malicious ritual of the Horse's Head, which is definitely not Christian,

> "Here I set up a 'pole of insult' against King Eirík and Queen Gunnhild' – then, turning the horses head towards the mainland – 'and I direct this insult against the guardian spirits of this land, so that every one of them go astray, neither to figure nor find their dwelling places until they have driven King Eirík and Queen Gunnhild from this country." (Nordal 1933) [53].

The magical 'spell' inherent in the language is reinforced not only graphically but in physical terms to give ritually added weight to transfer the destruction of his enemy; it thus forms a type of intertextuality – both text/runic and physical/visual. *Gunnhildr's* reply was to urge *Eirík* to kill *Egil* for such a heinous and an abhorrent act, stopping *Egil* from gaining his status and inheritance.

[48] Byock 1986: 161. Byock demonstrates the deep nature of Egils heathen beliefs.
[49] Einarsson, Stefán 1954, 1967, deduces from the palaeography structures that existed only at specific dates.
[50] Hoffman 2007.
[51] Clunies-Ross 2005: 32 Notices a specific example that was not in the original redaction illustrating a later date.
[52] Clunies-Ross 1989.
[53] Nordal 1933. This is a unique example of the vilification of a person and is clearly heathen.
[54] Túlunius' statement (2000, 530). Egil was totally against Christianity as an ultra-heathen it would have disrupted his beliefs and he would certainly not have been prime signed let alone converted.

Therefore, the writer does not agree with Túlunius' statement (2000, 530) [54], "The case of *Egill Skalla-Grímsson* is very interesting......because he is not quite a convert (to Christianity) and not quite a heathen either (?), having been prime-signed and his earthly remains are taken from a Heathen burial mound and moved to hallowed ground after the Conversion." It is this dichotomy that casts doubt on the narrative. This writer points out these facts were politically motivated by Snorri and others, *Egil* was an Ultra Heathen, therefore Snorri or his nephew have created a textual dichotomy,

(i) That inserting the text, 'prime-signed' was an addition to the saga, to improve *Egil's* standing for 13th century saga readership and make him viable for narrative inclusion into the Saga becoming a part of *Æthelstan's* court plus his presence at *Brúnanburh*.

(ii) It is noticeable that *Egil* has a pagan burial, his behaviour is 'head-on' Heathenism. The structural allusion of Christian empathy for *Egil's* behaviour is false, (a) he is totally Heathen in character, (b) the rehabilitation highlights a political correctness that 'bastardizes' the text.

Conversely, *Gunnar* was a Christian who attended *Æthelstan's* court and witnessed his charters. He was also a warrior skáld (poet) and because of his status may have had some input into the poem of *Brúnanburh*. Hill (2004 rept. 2011) [55] cites, J.D. Niles and M. Amodis (1989), who highlight skáldic technique in the *Brúnanburh* poem; they point out the similarity to *Hafsfjord*: 'clashing swords and crashing shields'; the term "*Iraland* for *Ireland*"; the word '*cnear*' for a warship (Scand. *Knorr* a sea trading vessel) and the use of kennings: 'spear-meeting or weapon-exchange'. Hill (2004 rept. 2011, 157-159) [56] explains, "all are thought to be strikingly original and Scandinavian in origin". *Gunnar Hlifrsson*, notice the use of the matronymic, was also a skald. This attribute had been passed down through his mother *Hlifr*, the daughter of *Jarl Törf Einar Rognvaldsson* This interesting attribute of skalds is noted by Barthi Guthmundsson (1967) in his book, *The Origin of the Icelanders*. As *Gunnar* was at *Æthelstan's* court could he have contributed to the poem in the Anglo-Saxon Chronicles? Such words would imply some Scandinavian imput.

However, *Egil* was definitely *Óðinn's* man not a Christian. *Egil's* whole behaviour, his aggressive, dark, violent character conflicts against this expression of Christianity. Snorri took over the estate of Borg in Iceland and wanted to show his pseudo-descent from *Egil* at the Norwegian court. Compare *Þórulf/Thorolf* in Egil's Saga with the historically recorded *Þórrøðr*: there is a remarkable similarity in their actions, both were killed in battle, and in contrast *Egil* and *Gunnar* survived (Blaney 1985[57]). Coupled with the previous discrepancies such remarkable closeness of plot and characters indicates a merger of two sagas.

The untrustworthiness of Egil's Saga is further exposed in a poem supposedly composed by *Egil* in *Æthelstan's* honour (Einarson Bjarni 1974 argues otherwise) [58]. It has this refrain,

"Now the Highlands, deer-haunted,
Lie humbled by Æthelstan."

---

[55] Hill (2004 rept. 2011) cites, J.D. Niles and M. Amodis (1989).
[56] Hill (2004 rept. 2011), 157-159. Hill notes specific Scandinavian words in the poem indicating a different hand.
[57] Blaney 1985: 343-53. The narrative runs parallel, Egil in the saga and Gunnar in historical charters.
[58] Einarson Bjarni 1974 argues otherwise.

This article questions whether *Egil* composed this refrain which 'smacks' strongly of *Æthelstan's* invasion of Scotland in AD 934. It is most definitely **not** *Brúnanburh* in AD 937, which was fought in Northumbria. Snorri or his nephew have taken this refrain from what appears to be yet another saga, a type of intertextuality; what Umberto Eco[59] calls *'intentio operis'* the intention of the work (Eco 1992: 66; Túlunίus 2000 p 527, cites Todorov 1970, see page 12 of this article)[60]. Therefore, Snorri or others attempt to deceive the reader that Egil fought at *Brúnanburh*.

Egil's Saga states, 'Every Norwegian had been gathered together in a column, with *Thorolf* as the leader.'[61] No mention is made of Christian Danes of the Danelaw or Danish influence and this appears to be yet another confused interpolation by Snorri or others to curry favour with the Norwegian court with which he had numerous political dealings. This Norwegian column is *highly unlikely* to have been employed by the pious *Æthelstan*. In addition, *Egil* had killed *Eyvind the Shabby* and was outlawed from Norway. Note his brother *Þórulf/Thorolf's* statement, "After what you've just done," said *Thorolf*, "it wouldn't be wise for us to go back to Norway this autumn!" (Egil's Saga).

Again, most of *Egil's* fighting was done in the east *not* the west (see Rafn 1859 who discusses the travels of the brothers in Courland)[62]. Chronologically these events came after the battle of *Brúnanburh*. The inference of Egil's travels highlights the fact that he clearly falls into the Heathen Camp and he was elsewhere rather than at *Brúnanburh*.

These above points highlight major discrepancies in the plot of Egil's Saga. They demonstrate the strife between the Heathens and the Christians. Also, they point in a different direction, rather than *Egil*, they indicate that *Gunnar Þórrøðrsson* aka *Hlífrsson* was the person concerned, whose family were staunch Christian.

Christian characteristics and Continental Kings dominated the Kings entourage, inherently a mixture of political, social and cultural aspects at *Æthelstan's* court, as such it would be an anathema to *Egil*, he would not have been able to deal or live with such a situation. As we shall see below. We must note *Gunnar's* eldest son *Þórrøðr* becomes the Christian Jarl of York, *Jarl Þórrøðr Gunnarsson* is mentioned in *ASaxChron AD 966; Ailred of Rievaulx Twysden col 362, 372, EAF j687*[63].

PRIOR TO 'THE GREAT BATTLE'

Æthelstan's status as a great king was measured thrice, not only from (i) the Battle of *Brúnanburh* but (ii) from his previous conflicts supporting his father Edward the Elder and (iii) from his Christian influence controlling the various petty kings of Britain to pursue friendship and peaceful diplomacy. This policy was pursued internationally by forming marriage alliances with the three immediate kingdoms to the east of England – Flanders, Francia and Germany.

---

[59]. Eco 1992: 66. Umberto's analysis of narrative and its relationship to character showing intent is most important.
[60]. Túlunίus 2000 p 527, cites Todorov 1970.
[61]. Egil's Saga.
[62]. Rafn 1859 Rafn is quite illuminating dating Egil's travels in Courland and the East to the time of Brúnanburh.
[63]. *Ailred of Rievaulx Twysden col362, 372, EAF j687*.

This attitude brought about a change from the old heroic style of kingship by creating an intellectual elite, bringing about a planned structured organisation with an 'end game' for each policy. Other kings realised they wanted to be associated with these new ideas, for it offered stability, an ordered govenance. On this wider political stage, *Edgiva*, daughter of *Edward the Elder* fled France with her son *Louis* after her husband *Charles the Simple* was imprisoned. Æthelstan continued to look after them as his father had done.

In AD 926 the Duke of the Franks, *Hugues* the son of *Robert*, approached *Æthelstan* to not only to ask for Louis to return to France as King but also to ask for *Æthelstan's* sister's hand in marriage Ethilda / Eadhild. *Hugues* was of the opposing camp that had dethroned *Charles the Simple*, so proceedings (AD 933/4) were delicate but he succeeded with conditions stipulated by *Æthelstan*, who forced *Hugues*, plus his embassy under oath, that '*Louis* would have the homage of all his vassals, and would show good Christian and honourable intent'. It should be stated that *Hugues* did not want to be king *"for Hugh recalled that his father had lost himself by too much presumption, and this memory made him dread reigning."* So, it was with great humility that *Hugues* approached *Æthelstan*. Clearly, *Æthelstan* recognised this aspect in *Hugues* and by his attitude responded with a regal status on an international scale being submitted to as an important Christian King. The moral emphasis can be seen in the following extract, an aspect that Egil would not have understood. This interesting passage about *Æthelstan's* court (c. AD 933/4) was written later in the 10th century by Richer of Rheims (taken from, *Histoire de son Temps Vol 1* trans. J. Guadet 1865, p121-125)[64]:-

I. *Les Gaulois délibèrent sur le choix d'un roi (936).*

Après les funérailles du roi Raoul, les grands se divisèrent et portèrent leurs voeux de divers côtés. Les Celtes et 1m Aquitains tenaient pour Hugues, fils du roi Robert; les Belges pour Louis, fils de Charles. Mais ni Hugues, ni Louis n'avaient lieu de rechercher le trône, car Hugues se rappelait que son père s'était perdu par trop de présomption, et ce souvenir lui faisait redouter de régner. Louis, de son côté, habitait alors TAngleterre, où il avait été porté encore enfant près du roi Adelstan, son oncle; poursuivi qu il était par Hugues et Herbert, qui avaient saisi et emprisonné son père. Les Gaulois donc, voulant paraître entiireinenl libres dans l'élection de leur roi, se réunirent pour en élire un sous la présidence du duc Hugues.

II. — *Discours de Hugues aux Gaulois en faveur de Louis.*

Après longue délibération, le duc, inspiré par des sentiments de bienveillance, se plaça au milieu de l'assemblée et parla en ces termes: « Le roi Charles est mort dans le malheur, sour qu'il y ait eu de sa faute, soit que notre conduite ait mérité la colère de Dieu. Si nos pères ou nous, avons offensé la Majesté Divine par nos actions, employons, avant tout, nos efforts pour en effacer la trace et la dérober aux yeux. Que tout sentiment de discorde disparaisse donc et délibérons d'un commun accord sur le choix d'un chef.
Mon père, jadis créé roi par votre volonté unanime, ne put régner sans crime, piusque celui qui seul avait des droits au trone vivait, et vivait enfermé dans une prison, ce qui, bien certainement, ne pouvait etre agréable au ciel. A Dieu ne plaise donc que j'occupe la place qu^eut mon père! Je ne pense pas non plus qu'après Raoul, de sainte mémoire, on doive porter au trône un homme de race étrangère, car ce qu'on a vu de son temps pourrait se reproduire encore: savoir, le mépris du roi , et , par suite , les dissensions des grands. Rappelez donc la lignée quelque temps interrompue de la famille royale; rappelez d'outre-mer Louis, fils de Charles,

---

[64.] Richer *Histoire de son Temps Vol 1* trans. J. Guadet 1865, p.125. This is the earliest source for Rollo - 10th century.

et ne craignez pas de vous le donner pour roi. Par là sera conservée l'antique noblesse de la race royale; par là cesseront les plaintes de ses partisans. Faisons donc ce qu'il y a de mieux à faire et rappelons le jeune homme d'au delà des mers. Les princes gaulois accueillirent ces paroles avec la plus grande faveur. Le duc expédia alors à Louis des envoyés éloquents' pour l'engager, au nom du duc des Gaules et des autres grands, à revenir parmi eux; pour lui garantir, sous serment, sûreté pendant leroyage et lui Annoncer que les princes viendront aa devant de lui jusqu'au bord de la mer. Les envoyés étant ptrtis se rendirent à Boulogne; ils s'embarquèrent dans ce port, un vent favorable enfla leurs voiles et ils touchèrent proniptement la terre.

Le roi Adelstan était au milieu des siens dans la ville nommée Eurvich, ou il s'occupait, avec son neveu Louis, des affaires du royaume. Les envoyés s'y étant rendus abordèrent le roi et le saluèrent honorablement de la part du duc et des seigneurs des Gaules.

III. — Ambassade de Gaulois au roi Adelstan pour lui demander Louis.

Les envoyés, faisant connaitre au roi leur mission, lui dirent: Les bonnes dispositions du duc et des plus puissants d'entre les Gaulois nous amènent ici à travers les eaux d'une mer inconnue, tant sont grands et unanimes la volontè et le consentement de tous. Raoul, de sainte mémoire, ayant été enlevé au monde, le duc a fait reconnaitre Louis pour son successeur, bien que plusieurs n'aient donné leur assentiment qu'aves peine, parce que, complices de l'arrestation du père, ils parce que, complices de l'arrestation du pere, ils se mefiaient (méfient) de fils. de fils. Cependant les efforts du duc les ont tous amenés à consentir avec joie. Tous désirent donc, par-dessus tout, posséder Louis, et ils n'ont rien de plus cher au monde que sa conservation; tous vous demandent de leur rendre celui qu'ils désirent voir régner dans les Gaules pour le bien commun. Ils demandent qu'on fixe le moment ou le duc et les prines pourront venir jusqu'au bord de la mer audevant de leur roi futur.

Adelstan n'ayant peut être pas assez de confiance dans des étrangers, leur demanda d'engager leur foi par serment; ils se rendirent à ses désirs, et l'on fixa un jour pour s'entendre. Les envoyes quitterent le roi, chargesde presents, se remirent en mer et revinrent dans les Gaules, apportant au duc les remerciments d'Adelstan et l'assurant d'une vive amitie de la part de ce roi pour avoir rappele Louis au trone.

Le duc et les princes des Gaules vinrent donc à Boulo(;ne pour y attendre le roi, leur seigneur. Ils se réunirent sur le bord de la mer et mirent le feu à des cabanes pour annoncer leur présence à ceux qui étaient sur le rivage opposé. Le roi Adelstan s'v trouvait avec sa cavalerie royale, disposé à envoyer son neveu aux Gaulois, qui Tattendaient; quelques maisons incendiées par son ordre montrèrent aux nôtres qu'il était arriré.

Adelstan envoie donc en ambassade aux Gaulois places i Topposite Tévcque Odon , qui fut plus tard archevêque de Cantorbëry *, homme juste et éloquent^ il leur faisait dire qu'il leur accorderait Louis volontiers, si Ton devait lui rendre, dans les Gaules, autant d'honneur que luimême en avait reçu chez lui , les Gaulois ne pouvant moins faire en effet ; et il demandait qu'on s'y engageât par serment; que si l'on s'y refusait, Louis recevrait de lui une partie de ses royaumes , où il vivrait content au milieu de ses sujets sans être importuné de sollicitations étrangères. Le duc promit, ainsi que les autres seigneurs des Gaules, qu'il ferait ce qu'on demandait, si Louis, devenu roi , con- WDtait à suivre ses conseils; en conséquence, il ne refusa point le serment. L'envoyé s'en retourna vers le roi, qui l'attendait et lui rapporta tout cela. Adelstan, rassuré, fit embarquer, avec un grand déploiement de pompe, son neveu Louis, accompagné des hommes les plus puissants du pays.

Translation (J.R. Kirby 2017):

I - The Gauls deliberate on the choice of a king (AD 936).

After the funeral of King Raoul, the great ones divided and carried their vows from different sides. The Celts and Aquitans were for Hugh, son of King Robert; The Belgians for Louis, son of Charles. But neither Hugh nor Louis had any occasion to seek the throne, for Hugh recalled that his father had lost himself by too much presumption, and this memory made him dread reigning. Louis, on his side, then lived in England, where he had been worn still a child near King Adelstan, his uncle; pursued that it was by Hugues and Herbert, who had seized and imprisoned his father. The Gauls, therefore, wishing to appear free in the election of their king, to elect one under the presidency of Duke Hugues.

II. – The speech of Hugues aux Gaulois in favour of Louis.

After long deliberation, the duke, inspired by feelings of benevolence, stood in the midst of the gathering and spoke in these terms: "King Charles died in the misfortune, whether there has been his fault, or whether our conduct has merited the wrath of God. If our fathers, or ourselves, have offended the Divine Majesty by our actions, let us employ, above all, our efforts to erase the trace of it, and to annul it. Let every feeling of discord disappear and let us agree on the choice of a leader. My father, once created by your unanimous will, could not reign without a crime, even if he alone had rights to the throne, and lived in a prison, which certainly could not be agreeable to heaven. So God forbid that I occupy the place which my father had! I do not think so no more than after Raoul, of holy memory, one must to carry to the throne a man of foreign race, because this which has been seen in his time, could still be reproduced: The contempt of the king, and, consequently, the dissensions big ones. Remember the lineage some time interrupted by the royal family; Remember from overseas Louis, son of Charles, and do not be afraid to give it to you for king. This will preserve the ancient nobility of the royal race; in this way will cease the complaints of his partisans. So, let's do the best thing to do and remember the young man from beyond the seas. The princes Gauls welcomed these words with the greatest favour. The duke then sent to Louis some eloquent envoys for in the name of the Duke of Gaul and other great men, at returning among them; to guarantee him, under oath, security during the journey and announce that the princes will come to in front of him to the edge of the sea. The Envoys sent gone repaired to Boulogne; they embarked from this port, a "favorable" wind in their sails and touched the earth. The King Adelstan (Æthelstan) was in the area / middle of his own town called Eurvich (York), where he occupied himself with his nephew Louis, with affairs of state.

III. - Embassy of Gauls to King Adelstan to ask him Louis.

The envoys (messengers/diplomats) who attended the King there and saluted him with honours / honourably on behalf of the Duke and the nobles / lords of France bring us here through the waters of an unknown sea, so great and unanimous are the will and the consent of all.

Raoul, of holy memory, having been removed from the world, the duke has had Louis recognized for his successor, although many have given their assent, because, accomplices of the father's arrest, they are mistrust (suspicious) of sons. Yet the efforts of the Duke have all led them to consent with joy. All desirent therefore, above all, to possess Louis, and they have nothing more dear to the world than its (his) preservation; all ask you to give back whatever they wish to reign in (over) the Gauls for the common good. They demand that the moment when the duke be fixed, and the princes may come to the edge of the sea before their future king. Adelstan, (Æthelstan) having perhaps not *sufficient confidence in strangers, asked them to pledge their faith by sacred oath; they surrendered to his desires, and they fixed one day to hear each other. The envoys left the king, loaded with presents, returned to the sea, and returned to the Gauls, bringing to the duke the thanks of Adelstan, (Æthelstan) and assuring him of a strong friendship on the part of this king for having recalled Louis to the throne.*

The duke and the princes, of the Gauls therefore came to Boulogne to wait for the king, their lord, and they assembled on the shore of the sea, and set fire to huts to announce their presence to those on the shore King Adelstan was with his royal cavalry, ready to send his nephew to the Gauls, who were waiting for him, and some houses, burned by his order, showed to our own that he had come.

Adelstan sends in embassy to the Gauls placed I Topposite Tévque Odon, who was later Archbishop of Canterbury, a just and eloquent man, That he would grant them willingly, if Return to him, in Gaul, as much honor as himself had received at his house, the Gauls could not less do indeed; and he demanded an oath;that if it were refused, Louis would receive from him a part of his kingdoms, where he would live contented among his subjects, without being importuned by foreign solicitations. The duke promised, along with the other lords of Gaul, that he would do what was asked, if Louis, become king, he had to follow his advice; consequently, he refused the oath. The envoy returned to the king, who awaited him and reported all this to him. Adelstan, reassured, made embark, with a large deployment of pomp, his nephew Louis, accompanied by the most powerful men in the country. They put to sea, by a favorable wind which swelled and the foamy oars led them peacefully to Tarre. The ships being tied to the shore, Louis went out, and welcoming the duke and other persons.

It is the tone of this speech by *Duc Hugh* to *Æthelstan* that is courteous and respectful but also humble for indirectly it reveals more about the turmoil of French politics at that time; also, it demonstrates the political power that *Æthelstan* was able to wield.

The socio-politics of AD 933/4, three years before the battle of *Brúnanburh*, highlight Christianity and international policies on a wide scale. This is all the more surprising as the court of *Æthelstan* travelled from place to place around England. Even though the main base was at Winchester various scriptoriums were also to be found in York, Worcester, Litchfield, Malmesbury, Peterborough etc. Many scholars comment on Vikings raiding for plunder and settlement being regarded as heathen pirates and that political conquest of areas such as the Danelaw, the duchy of Normandy plus the kingdom of Dublin were by heathen Scandinavians. However, it should be pointed out that many of these Scandinavians were actually converted to Christianity. Many in the Danelaw were descended from the Danish Royal House and were already converted c. AD 826/830 before arriving in this country. This raises the argument that there was religious division within the Scandinavian society. Sawyer (1997 p94) states that whereas, "we must infer that many raids have gone unrecorded ….we must not push this too far and make the Vikings out to be more effective than they were." It is this argument that needs to be fully explored. Seen as the 'arbiter' of Europe, *Æthelstan* had many continental Kings sons at his court in York c. AD 933/4, *duc Louis*, the future *king Louis IV (Outremer)* of France, the son of *King Charles* and *Edgiva* daughter of *Edward the Elder* and sister to *Æthelstan*. Other nobles were Breton – *Alan Forkbeard*, Germanic – *Otto* future King and Emperor, son of *Henry*, and Norwegian - *Hákon (the Good/ Aðelstansfóstri)* future King and son of *Harald Finehair*. Even earlier *William Longsword, Count of Rouen* (c. AD 893-17th Dec 942) was present at *Æthelstan's* court, the son of *Rollo*, son of *Rögnvald, Jarl of Møre* and *Romsdal. Rollo*, 1st Count of Rouen (c. AD 846 - c. AD 930/1) had been converted to Christianity in AD 912 and took the name Robert, being baptised with his son William by Franco, the Archbishop of Rouen[65]. Clearly, Egil could not have lived with this company at *Æthelstan's* court.

Figure 4. British Library "The miniature shows the baptism of Rollo (b. c. AD 846, d. c. AD 931), the founder of the Norman dynasty, and his marriage to Gisella, daughter of Charles III. Both events sealed the Treaty of Saint-Clair-sur-Epte (AD 911) in which the French king granted Rollo lands in Neustria in exchange for his feudal allegiance. Numerous portcullises of the Beauforts, which Henry VII adopted as his badge (his mother was Margaret Beaufort), and the royal arms decorate the borders of the text". https://www.bl.uk/catalogues/illuminatedmanuscripts/TourHistoryVernac.asp
Creative Commons CC0 1.0 Universal Public Domain Dedication.

---

[65] Chron.de St Denis, iii 99, (also Royal 20 E ii f.33, *Grandes Chroniques de France*).

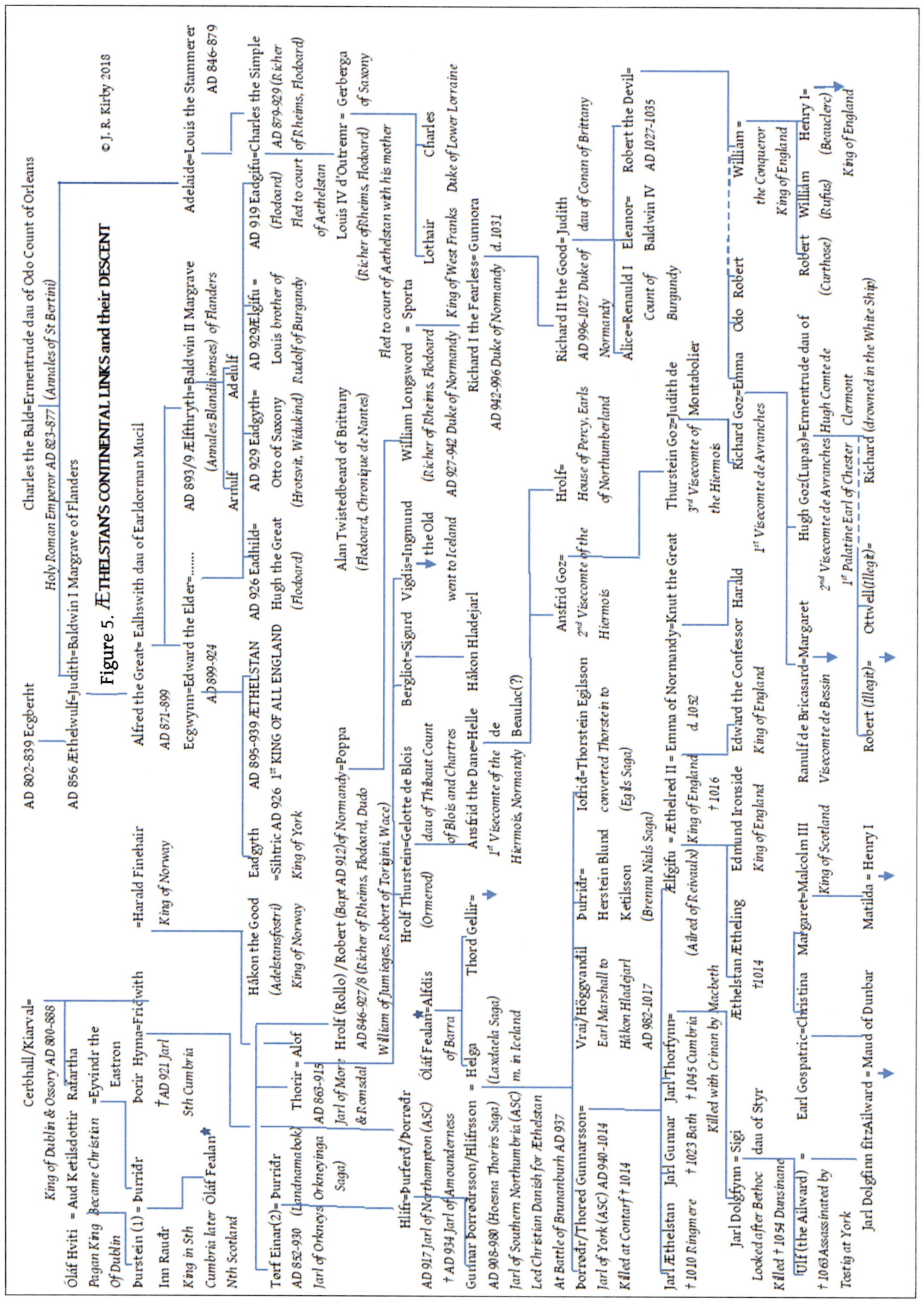

Figure 5. ÆTHELSTAN'S CONTINENTAL LINKS and their DESCENT

THE CHRISTIAN BEHAVIOUR OF ÆTHELSTAN

Thus, the Christian court of *Æthelstan* was in extremely stark contrast to *Egil's* Ultra Heathen beliefs. This was the company that *Jarl Þórrøðr Þórusson,* his son *Jarl Gunnar* and wife, *Hlífr* daughter of *Queen Þurriðr* and *Jarl Törf Einar Rognvaldsson*[66] chose to keep. Interestingly, this implies that *Törf Einar* was probably in contact with *Edward the Elder* and *Æthelstan*, although there is no concrete evidence available. Could the policy of *King Harald Finehair* (c. AD 850 – c. AD 932) and his son *Hákon Aðalsteinsfóstri* (AD 920-961) have had an impact on *Törf Einar*. Certainly, his elder brother *Hrolf Rognvaldsson* (Rollo, 1st Count of Rouen) had converted to Christianity. This author suggests it may have had economic and trade implications, as well as forming continuity and a stabilised authority for both Orkney and Normandy. Notable, is Gunnar's son in law, Hjalti and Gizzur the White bringing Christianity to Iceland in the year AD 1000, thus finally changing the old order. The old Heroic Ideal was giving way to an intellectual organised governance. The Christian *Jarl Þórrøðr Þórusson* had married *Hlífr, Törf Einar's* daughter and *Gunnar Þórrøðrsson* (aka *Hlífrsson*) was born c. AD 910, this was certainly within the chronology of *Törf Einar's* life. There are various dates for *Törf Einar's* death but between AD 920-8 seems to be acceptable. Indeed, the *Rognvaldssons: Einar* and especially *Rollo* seem in the latter part of their lives to be entertaining Christianity, (see *Flodoard AD 928 and AD 933 who mentions Rollo, Jarl of Rouen and his son William Longsword being present at Æthelstan's court*), for legal governance and social respectability was their *modus operandi,* thus establishing and sustaining their dynasties, as a consequence forming links with other powerful dynasties. *Hákon Aðalsteinsfóstri* the youngest son of *King Harald Finehair* was at *Æthelstan's* court as his name implies. He would have had no love for Egil, who had killed his brother, apart from this aspect he was a Christian. Most noticeably when he became King of Norway he was known by the title of *Hákon the Good* (see *Þórulf /Thorolf's* statement on page 26 of this article. *Egil* had killed *Eyvind the Shabby*.). Here is another dichotomy between Egil's Saga and historical fact and a lack of awareness of the impact of the new Christian order on the international political stage.

"With the help of Christ they had the victory." In the 'F' version of the Anglo-Saxon Chronicle derived from the 'E' version there is this passage, "*Her Æðelstan cing and Eadmund his broðer lædde fyrde to Brunan byri . . . and (Crist)e fultumegende sige hæfde,*" the compiler most probably used an MS from a lost Winchester record according to Campbell (1938: 149-50, app. 4.A.2 "Notices of the Battle Not Derived from the Poem"), he highlights the above phrase acknowledging that it was through Christ who had helped them gain the victory. Christianity was always at the forefront of *Æthelstan's* mind along with its impact on socio-politics. Just before the battle *Æthelstan* gave a prayer, which may have been delivered in front of his army. It is believed to have been preserved in the *Cotton MS Nero A. ii, f. 10v-11v, Carta Dirige Gressus; f. 11v-12v* and in *Cotton MS Galba A 14* are further evidence[67] that Egil's Saga was a mismatch of information.

[66.] See Johnston, A.W. (July 1916) "Orkneyinga Saga" *The Scottish Historical Review*. Vol. 13, No. 52. p393 [AD 910]. Muir, Tom (2005) *Orkney in the Sagas: The Story of the Earldom of Orkney as told in the Icelandic Sagas*. The Orcadian. Kirkwall. [AD 910]. Crawford, Barbara E. (1987) *Scandinavian Scotland*. Leicester University Press AD 910]. Crawford, Barbara E. (2004). "Einarr, earl of Orkney (fl. early AD 890s–930s)" [revised opinion AD 930]. Ashley, Michael (1998) *The British Monarchs*. Robinson Publishing [AD 920]; also, *Landnámabók* 1905.

[67.] British Library, London. *Cotton.MS Nero A. ii, f. 11*; see *Cotton MS Galba A 14*; also, Earle, J., ed. 1865. *Two of the Saxon Chronicles Parallel with Supplementary Extracts from the Others*. Oxford: Clarendon.; See Birch, Walter de Gray. (Ed.) 1885-1893. *Cartularium Saxonicum: A Collection of Charters Relating to Anglo-Saxon History*. Reptd. 1964. 3 Vols. [Vol. 2. pp332-2, Charters 656 & 657] New York and London. In Birch, the 'Prayer of Æthelstan' is in Latin and Old English.

The prayer before the battle of *Brúnanburh* was not mentioned in that saga; neither would *Egil* have accepted it nor listened as it was against his belief as an Ultra Heathen. It declares the following,

"Æla þu dryhten æla ðu ælmihtiga God . æla cing ealra cyninga . & hlaford ealra waldendra . on þæs mihta wunaþ ælc sige . & ælc gewin weorþ to bryt . for gif me drihten þ[æt] þin seo mihtigu hand mines unstrangan heortan gestrangie & þ[æt] ic þurh þine þa miclan mihte mid handum minum & mihte stranglice & werlice ongan mine fynd . winnan mæge swa þ[æt] hy on minre gisihþe feallan . & gereosan swa swa gereas Golias ætforan Dauides ansyne . þines cnihtes . & swa swa gereas & wearþ besenct Faraones folc on þære readan sæ . ætforan Moyses ansene . & swa swa feollan Filistei . beforan Israela folce . & swa swa gerias Amaleh . ætforan Moisen . & Chananei ætforan Iesu Naue. Swa feallan & gereosan mine find under minum fotum . & hi ealle samod þurh ænne weg ongan me cumen . & þurh seofan wegas hie fram me gewican; For bryt drihten heora wapna & heora sweord to bret & do drihten þ[æt] hy for meltan on minre gesihþe . swa swa weax mylt fram fyres ansyne . þ[æt] eall eorþas folc wite & ongyte þ[æt] ofer me is geciged noma ures drihtnes hælendes Cristes . & þ[æt] þin noma drihten sy geweorþad on minum wiþer winum . þu þe eart drihten Israela God."

Although the *MS Gaba A. 14* is accepted by Birch as being the genuine prayer spoken by *Æthelstan*, most modern scholars consider this as uncertain[68]. Ker (1957) dated it to early eleventh century or around 1000. However, *MS Nero A. ii* was earlier and thus has an aura of authenticity.[69] Therefore, this prayer may well be datable to the battle as it indicates the sincerity, devotion and piety of *Æthelstan* to Christianity; for he knew that many a kinsman, a friend, as well as an enemy would meet their deaths that day. His attention to the welfare of his men who followed him into battle placed an awesome responsibility on his shoulders as a devout Christian. The important aspect about this prayer is that it contrasts widely to the proceedings in Egil's Saga and undoubtedly *Egil* would not have considered their inherent virtuous attributes; but something *Æthelstan* would have considered most important as a characteristic feature of his chosen men. *Æthelstan* would have arranged his troops into specific cohorts, each cohort would have a shield wall and be from the same area as they knew one another's capabilities, with a bishop and captain. Thus, *Jarl Gunnar Þórrøðrsson* led the Christian men of the Danelaw into battle for *Æthelstan*, most probably in a shield wall wedge formation with spears poking through and the second wall of shields would be raised above the first with more spears poking through (this was similar to the Roman Armies 'Turtle').

Family tradition relates that *Gunnar* had a ring-sword called *Höggvanðil* - the hewing sword; this sword *Gunnar* gave to his second son, *Vrai*, who was called by this nickname - *Höggvanðil*. *Vrai / Höggvanðil* became *Hákon Ladejarls* Earl Marshall and was killed fighting in the Skåna region (see Savesjö Runestone in Småland). A strange parallel can be drawn between *Höggvanðil* - the hewing sword of *Gunnar* and *Egil's Dragvendil* – the trailing sword. One was used in battle to bring about honourable Christian good, the latter was used for Heathen enjoyment of vengeance. This seems to be a literary duplication but such 'ring-swords' did still exist at this time; the sword *Höggvanðil* had a *friðbond* which was attached to the guard or pommel ring and held the sword in its scabbard. The significance of the *friðbond* was that the weapon could not be used while the *friðbond* was attached, it fastened the sword in its sheath, keeping the *friðbond* attached in this way was a sign of peace and peace-making. Once realeased the sword would be 'out of peace'.

[68.] (Frances Rose-Troup, "The Ancient Monastery of Saint Peter and Saint Mary of Exeter," Transactions of the Devonshire Association, LXIIK1931). 218-219).

[69.] Ker, Neil R. 1957. *Catalogue of Manuscripts Containing Anglo-Saxon*. Oxford: Clarendon Press.

Another important aspect would be that *Egil* would not have the status or moral character to command the Christian cohort from the Danelaw. Jacobsson (2003 p15 n.8)[70] defines *Egil's* character,

> "The main difference between the childish Egil and the mature Egil is that the semi-psychopathic brutality of the child can be excused by his lack of maturity while the grown Egil really has no excuse. The uncontrolled aggressiveness of this 'hero' is more to be expected of the child than the man, and what makes the child Egil especially sinister is that his behaviour as a child, although it is on a smaller scale, is a fairly exact foretaste of his behaviour as an adult".

Jacobsson's (2003 p14) description of *Egil* rings true, "*His recklessness in getting his own way is nevertheless excessive and suggests an over-the-top mentality. Egil is represented as something of a sociopath, who does not care much about his fellow-man. What matters to him is to come out on top, to get even, to get his way*".

As "*an individualist, an existentialist, defining his own meaning in life, (Egil is) trying to form rational judgements regardless of living in what appears, to him as, an irrational universe*".

Figure 6. The battle triangle of three religions: Romano-British - Treales, Scandinavian – Lund and Christianity – Kirkham. All area divided by the 'Watling Street' derived from O.E. **wealhas** – foreigner. (© *Ordinance Survey of Great Britain New Popular Edition No.94 Preston 1945 1:63360*)[63]. CC granted 22nd Sept 2016, www.visionofbritain.org.uk

THE FYLDE: THE PLAIN OF DEATH

Interestingly, the split of *Anlaf's* (*Óláfr's*) army during the battle demonstrates that they were also arranged in groups: *Constantine's* Scots and Welsh contingents fleeing north and the Norse fleeing to their ships.

---

[70] Ármann Jakobsson 2003 *TROUBLESOME CHILDREN IN THE SAGAS OF ICELANDERS*. Saga Book Vol. xxvii Viking Society for Northern Research, University College London. See p.15 ft. 8. Jean-Paul Sartre in an interview with Morgunblaðið, 15th August 1951.

Tradition relates that a religious shrine was near to the battle site; this may have been a Roman, Heathen or Christian shrine or site. If the locale included all of these sanctuaries then the following place-names would be present: Temple, Altar; Lund, Grove; Ecclesia or Church. The line of a Roman road / street can be traced from North East of Preston on Fulwood Moor across to Lund and through Kirkham even on Victorian maps (see Ordinance Survey 1st Series Sheet 91SE Lancaster and Sheet 89 NW).

The opening battle was probably in the parish of Roseacre and Wharles. It is noticeable that the Scottish and Welsh forces are mentioned first in the poem retreating from the field of battle. There are two field-names that may show the scale of that disaster: Croneberry Fields, Cronebury Fields - the origin is Old Saxon but in also found in OScot: *Crone* – wail, lament, mourn derived from Old Saxon 8th century – 12th century; -berry, -bury, *byrig* – stronghold, OE: beorġe. ME: *Bergh*; Northern Dialect: *Berry/ Bury* – burgh, a fortified settlement.

These distinct field-names that betray the area of the initial battle where Æthelstan's army defeated the combined forces of the Hiberno-Norse and the Scottish and Welsh. The latter two groups, the Scottish and Welsh, were driven north along what is now known as Kates Pad but in those times'was Brythonic: *Catts Pad* (battle path). The Hiberno-Norse were driven along Danes Pad to Burn Naze (*Brúne Naes*) on the *Bergerode Peninsula*.

It seems that the names *Brúne* and *Bergerode* have been joined together to create *Brúnanburh* in Anglo-Saxon. It is because of this separate use of the names that scholars have been searching in vain for a complete name. Notice the *Annales Cambriae* describe the battle as "Bellum Brune" confirming the original name[71]. It is noticeable that the *Annales Cambriae* was written two years after the battle thus giving provinence.

THE 'PATHS OF THE DEAD'

The initial battle was fought some distance away from the ships at a place designated by the field-names: **Croneberry Fields** and **Cronebury Fields**. The importance of these names has been overlooked for in modern parlence they are thought to be derived from the fruit Cranberry c. AD 1500.

Yet, their true origin is much older dating from Old Saxon 8th century – 12th century: **cwáne** to lament, bewail, deplore or mourn – MidEng: *Croyne*; MLowGerm: *Kronen* – to moan, groan, lament. It is also found in Old Scottish: *Crone* – wail, lament, and mourn.

The suffix -berry, -bury, in the Northern dialect means, *byrig* – stronghold, OE: beorġe. ME: *Bergh*.

These by themselves would be interesting without any further substantiation for a stronghold used in the battle, but again we find other names: **Mote Field** – poss. OE: *(ge)mot* - a 'moot' or meeting place; **Northaws** – North ON: *haugr* - hill, barrow. These field-names are found in the Parish of **Roseacre** - ON: *hreysi* – field with a cairn, a heap of stones. 'They probably indicate the existence of a stone circle or burial mound', according to both Ekwall and Wainwright. Wainwright also identifies **Wharles** – OE: *hywrfel*, ON: *hvirfill* – a circle, ring.

[71.] *Annales Cambriae* 1860 Ed. Rev. John Williams Ab Ithel, p17.

All these names are just north of **Treales** - Old Welsh *Tref-llys* - the palace of the country folk (PIE: *treb*; OIrish: *treb*; OE: *ðorp* - home village), see F.T. Wainwright (1975 p.246). Described in the poem of the battle: ASC *ón folcstede* "on the country dwelling (estate) of the folk". Attached to this estate there are two field-names called **Chester** indicating that this was a place of importance during Romano-British times. Treales was the only name type in Northumbria that occurred in that disputed part of the ancient Kingdom of Rheged i.e. now western England – Lancashire. Rheged extended into Cumbria and the quickest yet most dangerous way was across firstly Pillings Mere then sandy mudflats of Morecambe Bay away from the battle for those who were familiar with the tidal changes. Many must have perished on this route if they were not cut down by Æthelstan's forces. Two famous scholars: J.R.R. Tolkein, who spent his holidays in the Kendal area[72]; a notable historian cum linguist, he was aware of some of these traditions, as was W.G. Collingwood. To use Tolkein's phrase "Paths of the Dead" the route across the Bay would bring them (those who had given their oaths in AD 927 at Eamont - now the 'oath breakers' in AD 937) across to an area generally known to locals on the Furness peninsula as the 'Vale of Nightshade' below Thursteins Vale.

The second part of the battle was fought at Burn Naze (DB) *Brúne Naes* on the *Bergerode* peninsula (now the Fleetwood peninsula) with easy access to the ships as the Heathen Norse were the most important to defeat, for it was they who instigated the opposing alliance of forces against Æthelstan. The field-names around Burn Naze betray this final battle ground. They consist of six field-names grouped together called **Borty Berry** – (*North. dial.*) berry - a burgh, an ancient fortified settlement. Borty – elder berry or in Northern dialect 'old' burgh. See Roseberry Topping, Northumberland. **Bottom Barty Berry** - (*North. dial.*) berry - a burgh, an ancient fortified settlement.

Immediately below these six fields, which are grouped together in a round shape, are eight field-names called **Arley** – ASax: *Ár-léas* (masc. nom.) – dishonourable, impious, wicked, cruel. See also **Marks Arley**, **Bottom Arley**, and **Lower Arley**. They are contained between two streams forming an area suitable for a battle. Immediately below these is an area (a holme) called Trunnah consisting of a number of fields named **Trunnah Field** – (*North. dial.*) round barrow/burial.

Explanation of the above field-names around Cronebury fields and Burn Naze demonstrates the furious battle over the types of ground. Both strongholds were placed on Holmes – islands on the plain. It is all the more amazing that for over a thousand years these field-names have remained the same.

By comparing the information, with the Amounderness / dingesmere argument we clarify the legitimate battle site locales of which there are two – initially in Roseacre and Wharles parish extending to Treales and lastly around Burn Naze, we are thus able to determine the correct locales. Pillings Mere is most interesting as the causeway across it was known as Kate's Pad (Brythonic: *Catt's Pad* – battle path). This causeway extended back to the Roseacre and Wharles Parish where the initial battle occurred. Along this causeway there are various burial mounds and this is probably where J.R.R. Tolkein (who had heard of the traditions of the area[72.]) derives his 'Paths of the Dead' in his novel, for it leads across the Morecambe Bay sands, treacherous at the best of times.

[72.] See Humphrey Carpenter 1977 *Biography of J.R.R. Tolkein*. Allen and Unwin.

The only piece of accurate factual information in Egil's Saga is 'a river running north', the only river that runs north in Northumbria is the last part of the river Wyre from Skippool to the Bay of Lune. This most probably came from the traditions of *Iófríð Gunnarsdóttir* who married *Thorstein Egilsson*. *Gunnar* and his eldest son *Þórrøðr* came back to this country, where *Þórrøðr* wasted Westmorland in AD 966 (ASC) becoming Jarl of York. *Gunnar's* second son was called *Vrai* by his family but *Gunnar* gave him his ring-sword called *Höggvanðil* - the hewing sword, hence the nickname given to him stuck in traditions. He became *Hakon Ladejarls* Earl Marshall and was killed fighting in Skåna where his name is carved on a runestone and it mentions his daughter. There was most probably a family saga written about *Gunnar* and his children as they were conspicuously important on a wider scheme of events which has been lost, noticeably mention is made in many famous sagas, in addition to *Höensa Þorirs Saga* which mentions *Gunnar's* character,

> "So ride they now to Woodstrand, to Gunnarstead, which lieth on the inner side of the Strand. There dwelt a man named Gunnar, the son of Hlifar, a big man and a strong, and the greatest of champions; he was wedded to a sister of Thord Gellir called Helga, and had two daughters, Jofrid and Thurid".
> *(from the 1891 translation into English by Eiríkr Magnússon and William Morris from the original Icelandic 'Hænsna-Þóris saga' in Chapter 10).*

> "Gunnar goes into Ornolfsdale, and Herstein (Blund Ketil) takes Gunnarstead. Then let Gunnar flit to him from the west all that timber which Eastman Erne had owned, and so gat him home to Ornolfsdale; then he falls to and builds up again the houses at the stead there; for he was the handiest of men, and in all things well skilled, the best of men at arms, and the briskest in all wise".
> *(ibid. Chapter 13).*

> "He went home to his house, and took his bow, for he was the best shooter among men, and came nighest therein to matching Gunnar of Lithend".
> *(ibid. Chapter 17).*

The contrast between *Egil's* character and that of *Gunnar* could not be more different. *Gunnar's* character traits and events in his lifetime would warrant a family saga, which has disappeared early on as *Gunnar* had returned to England with his eldest son. It was probably this lost saga MS that Snorri or *Saga Sturla* based the collation of Egil's Saga, in part, placing *Egil* at the forefront of the story rather than *Gunnar* in order to align himself with such important people. In the context of internationally important figures (see p.21 and 27 of this article) with *Æðelstan* it should be noted that *Egil's* character was in contradistinction to that of *Gunnar*. He would not have been tolerated at court; Jacobsson (2003 p.14 and p.15 n.8 see pp.30/1 of this article) defines *Egil's* character as uncontrolled aggressiveness, he does not care for his fellow man, selfish, reckless, and has a semi-psychopathic brutality.

The children of *Egil* and *Gunnar* show their respective father's status and relationships. *Thorstein Egilsson* marries *Iofrid* who had previously been married to *Thorodd Tungo-Oddson* indicating that *Thorstein* was still a Heathen but was influenced by Christianity. Later, when he marries *Iofrid* she converts him to Christianity against *Egil's* wishes. Further, *Thorgerd*, *Gunnar's* sister, marries *Skeggi* and their son *Hjalti* was instrumental with *Gizzur the White* in bringing Christianity to Iceland. Their approach was one of developed argument as opposed to *Thangbrands* violence – by killing any who disagreed with him. The link between *Hjalti* and his cousin, *Þórrøðr*, Jarl of York was economically and culturally important, developing trade routes for timber, lime, iron, livestock, cloth etc., between Reykjavik, Furness, York and Bergen in Norway. Obviously, this was very lucrative for we have evidence of Þórrøðr's wealth from an MS commissioned, it would seem, if the attribution below is considered of a holybook covered with jewels[73].

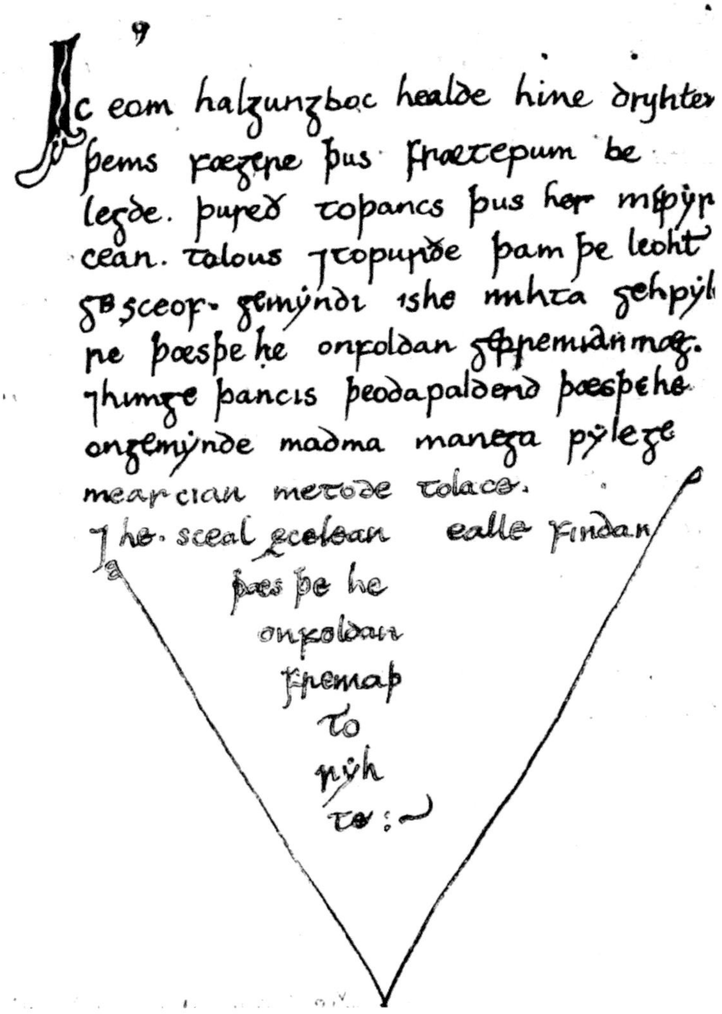

Ic eam halgungboc healde hine dryhten
þems faegtne þus fraetepum be legde. Þureð to þancs þus her míþyr
cean. Talous....

Figure 7. The only other *Thureth* of such importance was Þurferð / Þórrøðr Gunnarsson who became Jarl of York and whose father was a Jarl of Southern Northumbria, and whose daughter was the first wife of King Æthelred II. This 'halgungboc' (holybook) was probably written circa AD 980-1012. *Drawn from the facsimile from the Bodliean Library by J.R.Kirby 1998.*

The name Þureð / Þurferth mentioned here is the son of Jarl *Gunnar* who went over to Iceland to marry after the battle of *Brunanburh*. *Gunnar* married *Helga Óláfr Fealánsdóttir* and tradition was followed *Gunnar* naming his first son after his dead father. *Gunnar* was known by his mother's name *Hlifrsson* and is well recorded in many sources both traditional and historical. Because of his Norse grandfather Jarl *Tørf Einar Rognvaldsson* and because of the linguistic change his name became ON: *Þórrøðr*.

Therefore, the name of the grandson of Jarl Þureð / Þurferth was still employed showing that in scribal circles the name had not linguistically changed to the ON: *Þórrøðr*. Interesting to note is that *Helga Óláfr Fealánsdóttir's* brother was called *Þórð(Thored) Gellir*.

As both these families were Christian profitable trading routes were set up to Furness for lime and wood for building, sheep, wool, fruit, etc. Access to York as a major northern city was direct for precious metals and jewels, wine clothes, ivory etc.

[73.] *MSS Cotton Claudius A III*

D. Whitelock (1981 *History of Language and Literature in 10th & 11th century England.* London, XV, p217.) describes the *Wulfstan* 'hand' was that of *Wulfstan the homilist* (known as '*Lupas*' he died in AD 1023) and must not be confused with *Wulfstan I* who died in AD 956.

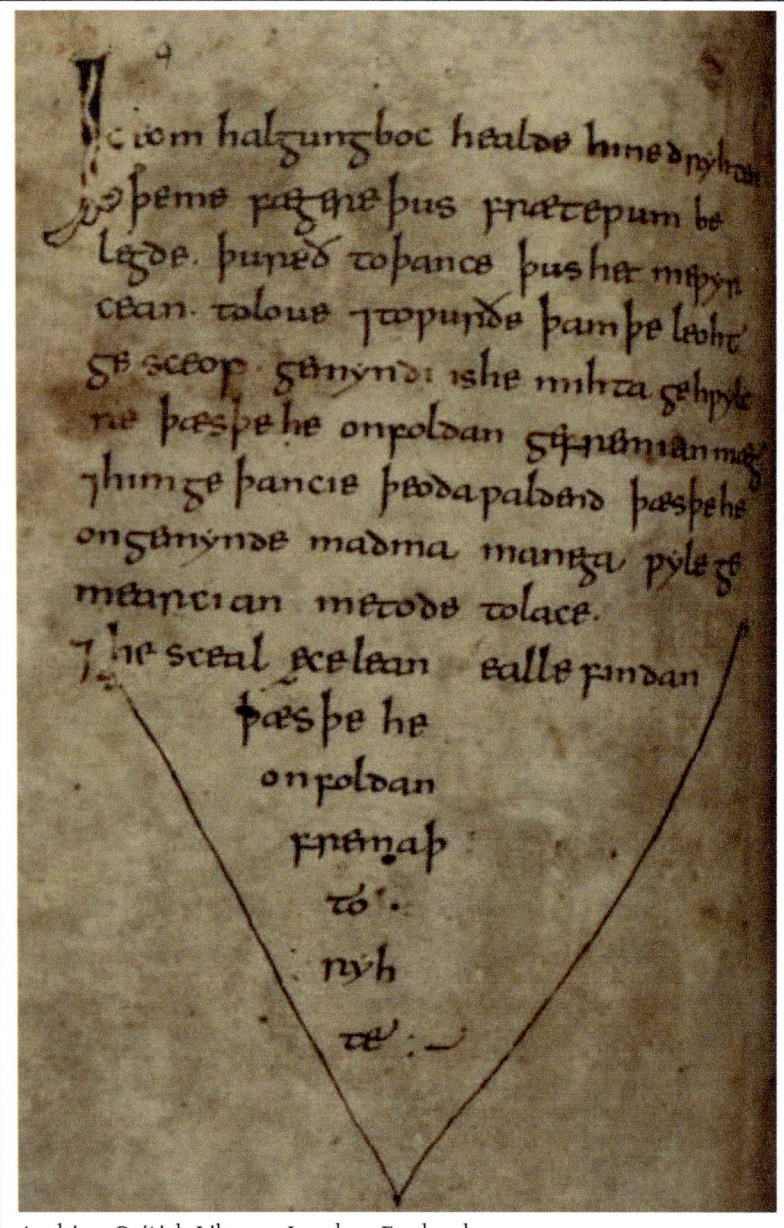

Archive: British Library, London, England
Shelfmark: MS Cotton Claudius A.III
Location f.31v
http://www.earlyenglishlaws.ac.uk/laws/manuscripts/k/?tp=s&nb=2797
"The Claudius manuscript is composite and only assumed its current form under the antiquarian Sir Robert Cotton in the seventeenth century. It contains three separate pontificals, the first two are eleventh-century manuscripts while the third was produced in the twelfth century".
© 2018 University of London -- Institute of Historical Research / King's College London. Email: earlyenglishlaws [at] sas.ac.uk

Figure 8. British Museum, Cotton Claudius A iii, ff 31v, Thureth. See No 185. [*Early English manuscripts in Facsimile Vol 23 Old English Verse Texts from many sources.* Ed. Fred. C. Robinson and E.G.Stanley. Rosenkilde & Bagger. Copenhagen. 1991].

See, Dobbie,E van K, 1942 *The Anglo-Saxon Minor Poems,* (The Anglo-Saxon Poetic Records, vi), Thureth, pp.lxxxviii-xc, 97, 193-4. "As the photograph shows, the text is offcentre and tilted on the page. The mark above the second word (eom) is apparently ink, possibly a false start on a letter. Marks above and to the right of this are holes in the vellum." Also, N.R.Ker 1957 & 1990 *Catalogue of Manuscripts containing Anglo-Saxon.* Oxford, p141 "An inscription and a set of 'sinodaeia decreta' of King Æthelred in Latin and OE versions occupy eight preliminary leaves (ff.31-38) of a benedictional written in caroline minuscule, s.xlxi." Ker identifies this Thureth as Þurferð / Þórrøðr Gunnarsson, Jarl of Northumbria. Further, see D. Whitelock 1981 *History of Language and Literature in 10th & 11th century England.* London, XV, p.217. "The presence in this part of Claudius A iii of the 'Wulfstan' hand makes unlikely the identification of the Thureth mentioned in the poem with Thored, a landowner who gave an estate at Horsley, Surrey, to Christ Church, Canterbury."

The Saga continues in its ambiguous vein. *Æthelstan*, according to Egil's Saga (Chpt 50),[74] asked *Egil* and *Þórulf /Thorolf* to accept "preliminary baptism, as was the custom in those days." In the light of *Egil's* complete Heathen character this chapter is dubious and stretches credulity. This appears to be an attempt to rehabilitate *Egil* into the Christian World.

Livingstone (2011)[75] states, '*Egil was a trusted warrior for Æthelstan*'. Yet, *Æthelstan* is unlikely to have used Heathen Scandinavian mercenaries to fight Heathens as mentioned in Chapter 50; *Æthelstan* would not have had them at court let alone in his army as they would need to prove their loyalty to him before he trusted them in battle. *Egil* 'appears' from nowhere, of unproven loyalty to *Æthelstan*, therefore Livingstone's statement is questionable. *Egil's prima signatio* (Nordal 1933:128)[76] may well be a later interpolation of the 12th century for it is a Latin phenomenon.

GENEALOGICAL EVIDENCE

Genealogical analysis. The important aspect to remember is that all these kinsmen of *Gunnar, Óláfr Fealán, Helgi the Lean* plus the descendants and followers of *Aud the Deepminded*, were of a Christian persuasion. Opposed to this ethos was *Egil Skalla-Grímsson* who was a Heathen. There were a number of children from the marriage of *Iófríð Gunnarsdóttir* and *Thorstein Egilsson*. (See Genealogical Analysis p.43). The relevance of genealogy highlights not only the chronological relationships but also the historical and socio-political analysis. It places the participants within the larger scale of events and clarifies the relationship between people in Iceland and those in England plus the location of the battle. It is important to note (see pp.22- 23 of this article) that Egil's Saga mentioned an unknown and ambiguous son of *Egil* called *Gunnar* – no such person exists, rather this was *Thorstein's* father-in-law, *Gunnar Hlifrsson*. The linage of *Þórrøðr Þórusson* and his son *Gunnar* can be traced through two recorded descents – the male line of *Thorfynnr Þórrøðrsson* descends to the present day in England and the female line of *Ælflaed Þórrøðrsdóttir* who was the first wife of *Æthelred II*. Both lines merge a few generations later when *Thorfynnr's* great grandson *Dólgfinnr* marries *Maud of Dunbar*. (See Appendix A – Christian Relationships). Helgason et al (2000, 2001)[77] have mapped the Icelandic populations DNA, especially the descendants of these early Scandinavians.

Recently, in 2006 Bryan Sykes (of Oxford Ancestors and Wolfson College, Oxford) has done specific analysis of those relations in England, compared them to those in Iceland and found a match of alleles belonging to the I1a haplogroup, especially when compared to Helgason et al (2000, 2001). So close is the match of alleles that those in England are one step earlier than those in Iceland, indicating direct descent. This haplogroup is unique to Denmark and Norway. Further, it should be noted that the various place-names in Low and High Furness correspond with Icelandic personal-names and these are not coincidence but are kinsmen and women of *Gunnar Þórrøðrsson*. They migrated to Iceland where they are called the Dalesfolk of the Western Fjords. Previously, there has been some dispute over the third son of *Jarl Þórrøðr Gunnarsson, Jarl Thorfynnr Mac Thore(d)*, in Manx he was called *Thoryn / Thor(f)yn*. This name *Thoryn*, a Manx etymology, does not mean that this was the correct pronunciation but there also seems to be a misspelling on the copy of the Gospatric Charter, as it should have been *Thored* not *Thore*.

[74.] Egil's Saga (Chpt 50)
[75.] Livingstone (2011)
[76.] Nordal 1933:128
[77.] Helgason et al (2000, 2001).

Neither is the ON name *Thorfynnr* unusual as *Gunnar's* mother was *Hlifr* the daughter of *Tørf Einar Rognvaldsson* Jarl of the Orkneys. *Jarl Thorfynnr the Mighty* of the Orkneys was *Jarl Thorfynnr Mac Thored's* cousin. The use of the Manx name *Thoryn* indicates a geographical link with the Isle of Man but interestingly *Thorfynnr's* son *Dólgfinnr* was travelling to Dublin – hence *Dólgfinnr's Barn* (*Dólgfinnr's* children) implying that some of his men were in Dublin and there appears to be economic and trading connections.

This continuity of family names continues as *Þórrøðr Gunnarsson* calls his eldest son after his father's friend *King Æthelstan*, then his second son is named after his grandfather *Gunnar* and the third son is named after his grandmother's kin *Jarl Thorfynnr the Mighty*, we should expect such names. This dispute was 'nailed' when Prof Bryan Sykes tested the DNA of the direct descendant of *Jarl Þórrøðr Gunnarsson*, it was found to have matching 'alleles' with those descendants from Iceland.

Socio-political events. The following aspects form a basic summary of the socio-political framework:

(i) Æthelstan bought Amounderness legally from a Heathen circa AD 933-934.
(ii) Purchasing Amounderness blocked the direct route from Dublin to York.
(iii) The AD 934 Nottingham Royal Charter was granted with the probability of a future conflict after the lack of recognisable compliance from the various sub-kings who submitted in AD 924 and again in AD 926 (see Stenton *Anglo-Saxon England*, p342).
(iv) Æthelstan gave Amounderness to Archbishop *Wulfstan I* of York and set *Þórrøðr Þórusson* in charge.
(v) *Þórrøðr Þórusson* was killed in battle fighting for Æthelstan on his Scottish invasion of AD 934. His name is commemorated on the Urswick cross. Geological comparison of the stones structure is compatible to the plinth in front of Kirkby Hall.
(vi) Both *Gunnar* and his father *Þórrøðr* were Christian Jarls of Amounderness.
(vii) The post of the cross is in Urswick church and illustrates the name *Torhtred / Þórrøðr*. This area of Furness was the home manor of *Þórrøðr Þórusson* as evidenced by the field-names. It was later confused with *Tostig Godwinsson's* manor of Hougen.
(viii) The Amounderness jarldom was the political pawn in the territorial dispute between Olafr and Aethelstan.
(ix) The lack of Danish evidence in Egil's Saga is revealing and illustrates the Christian Danes of the Danelaw were opposed to the Heathen Hiberno-Norse of *Óláfr*, the Scottish and the Strathclyde Welsh.
(x) The Strathclyde Welsh were involved as they saw Amounderness as part of their original kingdom – Strathclyde / Rheged.

Æthelstan's mercenaries were the Christian Danes of the Danelaw with their Mercian Allies. See *Armes Pryden Vawr*[78],

Vn cor vn gyghor a Lloegyr lloscit.
In a single party, of one mind with the Mercian (Welsh: *Lloegyr*) incendiaries,

---

[78.] *Armes Pryden Vawr*, (The Prophecy of Pryden the Great), from the *Llyfr Taliesin* (The book of Taliesin) Peniarth MS2 National Library of Wales.

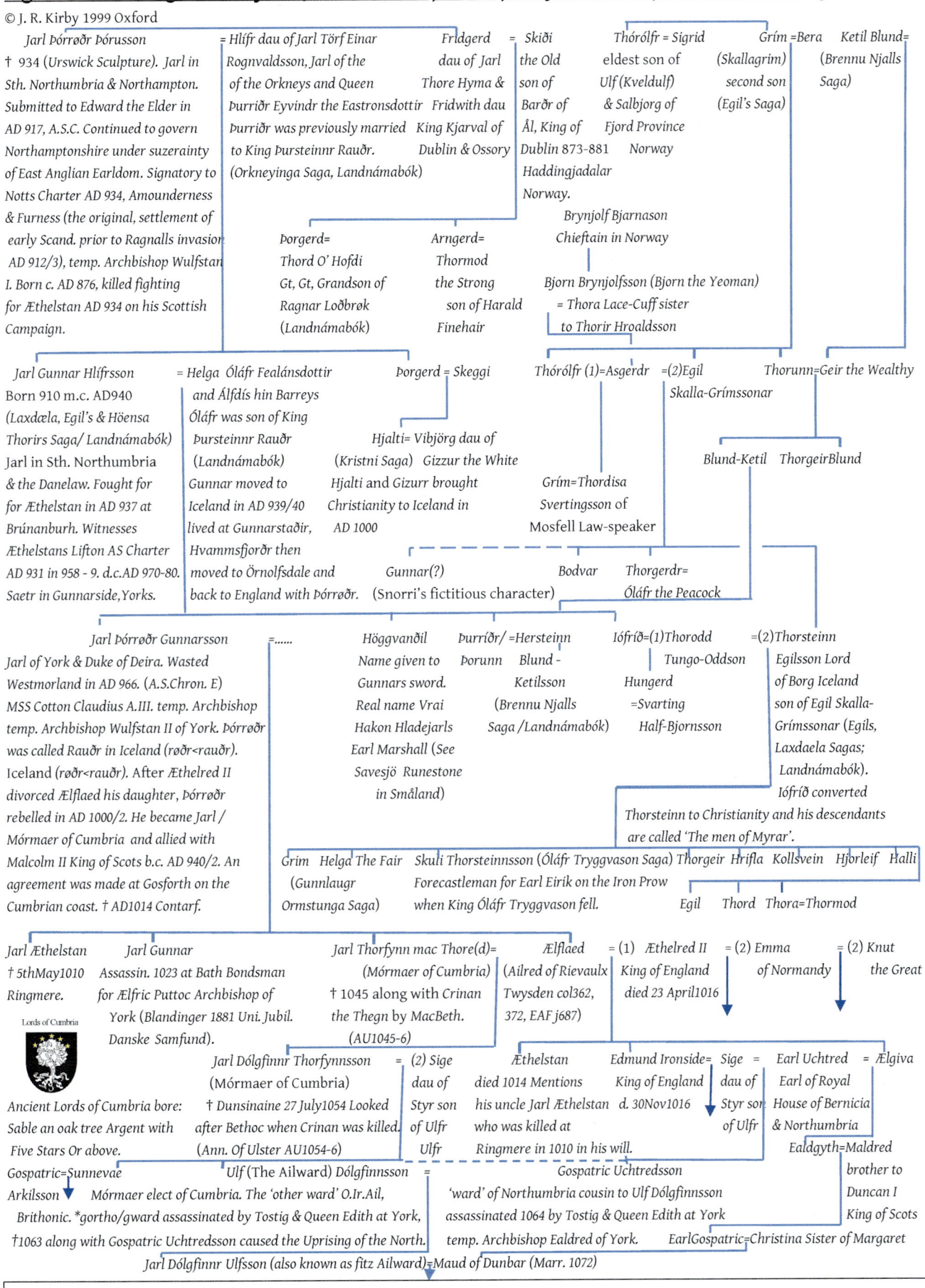

Figure 9. Genealogical analysis: *Jarl Gunnar Hlífrsson's family relationship with Thorsteinn Egilsson.*
© J. R. Kirby 1999 Oxford

See various historical charters and ecclesiastical deeds. Also *Landnámabók* Vigfusson and York Powell 1910 Vol.1 OUP; *Höensa-Þóris Saga, Brennu Njal's Saga, Egil's Saga, Kristni* and *Laxdaela Saga*, see *Íslenzk Fornrit*.

The 'Mercian incendiaries' included the men of the Danelaw. It should be noted that the first principle of the Danelaw, the Wapentake, was enacted; as the Jarldom of Amounderness was being attacked, all the other Jarls of the Danelaw came to *Jarl Gunnar's* aid. In this context, it is notable that the Brúnanburh poem states "the Mercian's did not refuse hard fighting". Understanding the socio-political events allows us to determine the key interest of all parties focused on the same territory. Jones (1952)[79], was not convinced that inconsistencies compared to historical sources may be accounted for in Egil's Saga. Yet, the charters of the period illuminate the people involved: *Æthelstan, Óláfr, Jarl Þórrøðr* of Northampton later Jarl of Amounderness; both he and his son *Jarl Gunnar* (who inherited the jarldom) were under their demesne lord, *Wulfstan I*, who was the Archbishop of St Peter's, York. Conspicuously, the area concerned, Amounderness (the Fylde region), is above the Ribble, within the kingdom of Northumbria (York) not at Bromborough which was in Merica. Crucially, *Gunnar* held the status of a jarl in this action at *Brúnanburh / BrúneBerg* - the harbour at Burn Naze (*Brúne Naes*) on Fylde. (See Kirby 2018)[80]. Notice also that the *Annales Cambriae* describes the battle as "*Bellum Brune*" confirming the original name[81]. *Gunnar* was the premier jarl of the Danelaw leading the Christian men of the Danelaw; as his jarldom was at the forefront of the battle he would have called the other jarls into action. We must therefore state that Amounderness had Danelaw borough status. This was one of the primary laws of the Wapentake in the Danelaw. This was why *Æthelstan* waited before starting the battle, the gathering of the army to the cry – ASax: *heire geleðian* (to the west assemble, this cry is from an old tradition in the Kirkby/Kirby family). ASax: *geleðian* later developed into *'leet'* – to give judgement. McDougall (1995)[82] discussed the 'ruse-story' – *Æthelstan* was stalling for time and reinforcements; however, onomastic and historical evidence highlight the *modus operandi* of the Wapentake – the weapon gathering, rather than the story employed in the novel.

Laurence de Looze et al 2015 4:57-75)[83] state of the narrative, "*Æthelstan's war against Óláfr at Brúnanburh may seem to be a digression is, I suspect, strategically placed in order to prepare for the York episode*". If this is the case for a fabrication of the narrative, one has to question the next statement, "*First, Egil does great service to Æthelstan particularly in relation to the recovery of Northumberland.*" This last statement goes against historical fact and is a complete fabrication as we have seen on the previous pages. Looze (2015 4:57-75) further compounds the confusion by stating, "*When Æthelstan subsequently grants Northumberland to Eirik he is giving the Norwegian a region that Egil effectively won for him.*" The incongruity to reality and fact is astonishing.

MARITIME AND LANDSCAPE ANALYSIS IN THE BRÚNANBURH MSS.

Germane to the comparison between *Brúnanburh* and *Egil's Saga*, is the argument that archaeological and scientific research has revealed a unique locale - the 'sea of noise' - one maintains the sea of noise, the other does not; also, the Amounderness coastline had navigable small creeks enabling a fleet of longships to be beached. Projected analysis by the Admiralty using the NASA database allows equinox data for the year (AD 937) to identify surges. (Kirby 2018[84]; British Crown Jan 2012, Admiralty, RN Nautical Almanac Office, Taunton. Lic. Ref. No. 557909[85] - see Appendix A).

---

[79] Jones (1952) "*Egill Skallagrímsson in England.*" Proceedings of the British Academy 38 (1952): 127–44.

[80] Kirby (2018) *Identifying Brúnanburh: ón dingesmere - the sea of noise.* Archaeopress.

[81] *Annales Cambriae* 1607 *Britannia* (trans.) Philemon Holland.

[82] McDougall (1995)

[83] De Looze, et al. 2015 *Egil the Viking Poet: New Approaches to Egil's Saga.* University of Toronto Press.

[84] Kirby (2018) *Identifying Brúnanburh: ón dingesmere - the sea of noise.* Archaeopress.

[85] British Crown Jan 2012, Admiralty, RN Nautical Almanac Office, Taunton. Lic. Ref. No. 557909.

Historical confirmation is found in the Annals of Innsfallen (AI 937, 151)[86] of extreme weather– a Low in the Irish Sea creating surge conditions above Chart Datum (Kirby 2018). The area to the south of the river Lune is described as the Fylde, derived from O.E. –gēfylde: gē 'district' and O.E. –feld, Mod. Eng. *fylde* 'plain'- the district of the plain, known also as Amounderness.

Landscape analysis of the poem pinpoints the region (**Feld/Fylde**) and the estate (**stede** of Treales Old Welsh *Tref-llys* - palace) of the country folk (**folcstede**) across to Fulwood Moor we are able to determine the initial battle and the later battle around (*ymbe*) Burn Naze (**Brúne** Pre-Domesday Book and *Annales Cambriae*). The battle was fought 303 years before Egil's Saga was collated in AD 1240 and *Bergerode* peninsula now called Fleetwood was only named in 1800-1810 after Sir Peter Fleetwood.

The two words **Brúne** and **Berg** were clearly joined – hence **Brúnanburh** (Kirby 2017) but this was only the second part of the battle. The initial battle was at the moor near Deepdale and Treales. Finding them was an outcome of topographical research, hence the identification problem of the locale. William Camden in 1607 emphasized a Northumbrian connection[87],

> *'uti Adelstanus eius filius nothus*
> *pleno ad victorias gradu multa*
> *Danorum caede Northumbriam*
> *debellavit, Danisque tanto terrore*
> *institit ut vel e regno excesserint*
> *vel se dederint.'*

It should be clearly emphasized that this is totally in keeping with the historical record about Burn Naze in Amounderness, which was in Northumbria, whereas Bromborough was in Mercia, specifically remarkable are the topographic phrases recorded in the primary source (see Evans 1997[88] who also highlights Danish men in Northumbria; see also Egil's Saga Chpt 51).

Noteworthy, are personal-names of the Icelandic Dalesfolk that are embedded in place-names found near most of the place-names in Amounderness and especially Furness, southern Cumbria; they correspond and confirm the same Dalesfolk families found in Iceland and England (see Kirby 2013).

---

[86] Annals of Innsfallen (AI 937, 151). (Unknown author) Ed. Seán Mac Airt. Corpus of Electronic Texts Edition. Funded by University College, Cork and Professor Marianne McDonald via the CELT Project.

[87] William Camden in 1607

[88] Evans 1997 *"Four Philological Notes."* Saga-Book of the Viking Society for Northern Research 24: 355-60.

Figure 10. Dalesfolk Names in Southern Cumbria

ON	*Ormr*	Ormsgill
ODan/ON	*Torhtred (Þórrøðr)*	Urswick Cross (Runic formally in front of 'Kirkby Crosshouse')
ON	*Gamall*	(KLM) Loppergarth Typanium, Pennington (Runic)
Anglo-Scand.	*Kilvert*	Killerwick
OES	*Steinarr*	Stennersley (see runestone on Barra in the Hebrides)[89]
Com Scand.	*Þrandi*	Trinkeld
Com Scand.	*Þúrsteinnr*	Thursteins Water (Coniston Water)
Com.Scand.	*Eyvindr/ Vinundr*	Windermere
Com. Scand.	*Gunnarr*	Gummers How
ODan/ON	*Stýrr*	Steers Pool
OIr.	*Beccan*	Beacons Gill
OIr.	*Ailéne*	Elliscales
ODan/ON	*Asmundr*	Osmotherley
ON	*Hrafn*	Ravensty
ON	*Finnr*	Finsthwaite
ODan/ON	*Hroaldr/Hrólfr*	Rusland
Gael.	*Beathag/Bethoc*	Bethecar Moor
ON	*Haukr*	Hawkshead
ODan/ON	*Arni*	Arnside
ODan/ON	*Toki*	Tock How
ON	*Hvelpr*	Whelpshead Crag
ODan/ON	*Blæingr*	Bleansley
ON/OIr	*Kiallakr/Cellach*	Croskelloc (near Ulverstone)
ODan/ON	*Eilifr*	Lower Allithwaite
ON	*Þorfinnr*	Thorfinsty Hall
OES	*Ulfarr*	Ewedale
ODan/ON	*Refr*	Roshead/Rosside(near Ulverston)
ODan/ON	*Kolr*	Colton

Unfortunately, other personal-names have been used in the saga and these have already been disproved highlighting the concoction of Egil's Saga i.e. *Hring* and *Adils*, legendary and heroic names (see Campbell 1971, 3,7[90]; also Cormack 2001, 61-68[91]; see also Bessason 1977[92] who speaks of 'mythological overlays'; for a negative view, see Túlunius 1994[93]).

---

[89] Stennersley (the runestone on Barra in the Hebrides states, *"Thorgerd raised this stone in memory of her father Steinarr"*). This occurred (c. AD 860-6) when King Þursteinnr inn Rauðr migrated up to North Scotland and linked with Sigurd Jarl of the Orkneys. Discussion with Prof Raymond Page and Prof Michael Barnes who also arrived at the same conclusion placing the date at circa AD 860-6 due to the structure of this sentence.

[90] Campbell 1971, 3,7

[91] Cormack 2001, 61-68;

[92] Bessason 1977

[93] Túlunius 1994).

Western dates		Einar Haugen's linguistic dates
Com Scand.	AD 600 – 860-6	AD 600 – 900 Yngre Urnordisk
OES	AD 860-6 – 1040	AD 900 – 1100 Olddansk
OWS	AD 860-6 – 1040	AD 900 – 1100 Vikingtiden
ON	AD 1040 – 1200	AD 1050 – 1350 Gammelnorsk

Many of the previous place-name arguments for *Brúnanburh* show an etymological similarity and because of a plethora of similar names in the north they are without any material evidence. Such arguments can be applied to *Bromborough, Brinsworth, Bourne, Bruneswald, Birrenswark* etc, and we return to the confusion of the 'place-name case'. Returning to the socio-political aspect, *Jarl Gunnar Þórrøðrsson* had left his jarldom of Amounderness, sailed to Iceland at this time AD 939-40, he was not available to gather the forces of the Christian Danes of the Danelaw to support Edmund, Æthelstan's successor. What is significant is that *Óláfr* in his later campaign attacks the Danelaw first rather than the prize of York, as retribution for their original involvement in the battle of *BrúneBerg*. The argument by *William of Malmesbury*[94] appears to have been confused with the second campaign against *Edmund* in AD 940. We now know many aspects of Egil's Saga to be fabricated by Snorri or his nephew who allegedly compiled this saga. Cormack's argument (2001, 64)[95] that "Snorri's authorship should not be taken for granted" is valid; to do so may be too absolute in the light of this above evidence. Also, Þórgeirsson (2014, 61-74)[96] not an advocate of the validity of Egil's Saga, points out on stylistic grounds, 'many hands are evidenced in the saga'. The ego of *Snorri, Óláf White-Poet* plus *Saga-Sturla* is still at the root of the problem plus the collation of traditions from different lost Saga's.

What emerges from the cautious approach of this article has turned some of the traditional arguments through its' different approach. It has brought out many new historical aspects that are verifiable which go against the traditional narrative of the saga. Consequently, it is the authors contention based on validated evidence that Egil's Saga cannot be used as a source for understanding the context of *Brúnanburh*.

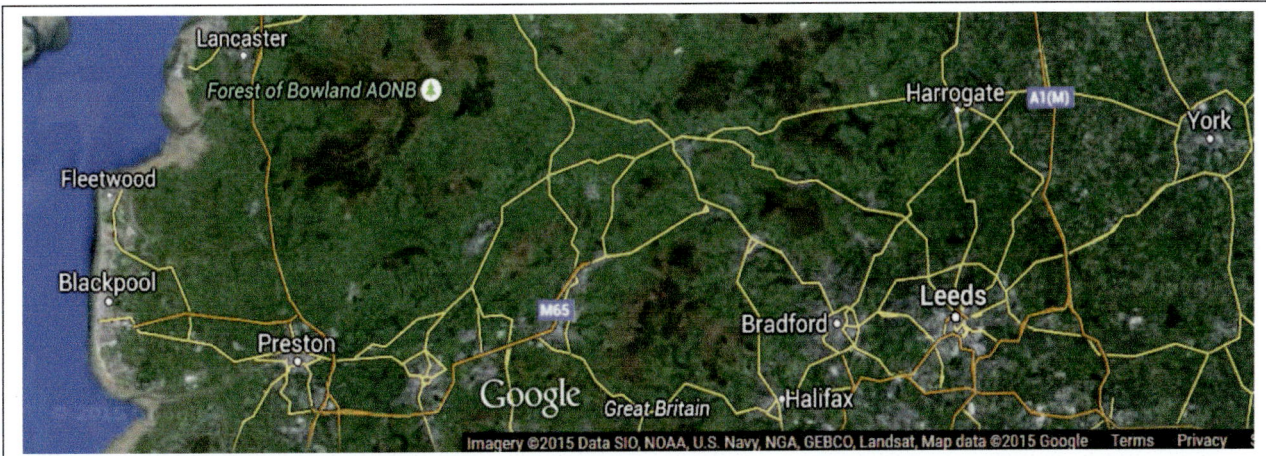

Figure 11. Amounderness is in a direct line on the Dublin / York axis. (*Imagery*©2015, Data SIO, NOAA, U.S. Navy GEBCO. Map Data © 2015 Google).

[94.] William of Malmesbury
[95.] Cormack's argument (2001, 64)
[96.] Þórgeirsson (2014, 61-74)

This author refers back to Campbell's (1938) statement[97],'*Unless new evidence can be produced, an honest nescio is greatly to be preferred to ambitious localisations built upon sand.*' This statement, by implication, applies not just to the reciprocity of *Brúnanburh* in Egil's Saga, when compared to historical sources but also to archaeological, geographical, place-name and genealogical evidence - the spatio-temporal/concrete against the paranormal/fantastic religious, supernatural, status framework mentioned in this papers rationale (see Túlunius 2000. 529 argument)[98]. The character of *Egil*, the man, is left in a dichotomy – he is an ultra Heathen but is made to look as a semi-Christian by Snorri or others.

While it is valid to say that *manuscript evidence is material culture,* in this case the Egil MSS is an exception to this rule as it was (a) collated three centuries after the event by either Snorri for self aggrandisement or (b) it was most probably written by the *Þordarssons*, Snorri's nephews c. AD 1241-1242. The collated work of Snorri highlights his socio-political self-advancement under the Norwegian court. Consequently, the saga is suspect and cannot be regarded as valid evidence for historical accuracy or of *Egil's* involvement in the battle. There are also considerable mismatches giving a false narrative.

Whatever arguments are arranged against these views expressed in this article, this fact remains: that the Christian *Jarl Gunnar Þórrøðrsson* (aka *Hlifrsson*) fought at *Brúnanburh* not *Egil*.

There is one other aspect that should be stated: that as Snorri did not finish Egil's Saga, noticeably there are a large amount of textual discrepancies, Snorri's writings must have been in 'note form' and not a coherent whole, this would account for such major discrepancies and the change of style demonstrated by Þórgeirsson. Therefore, we must look to *Óláf White-Poet* and *Saga-Sturla* for the composition produced after Snorri's death, creating the first redaction probably AD 1242/3. Thus, we can date the composition to 305/6 years after the battle of *Brúnanburh*.

There is a need to analyse and validate every piece of evidence, if one is to substantiate and arrive at the correct locale. It should be remembered that the topography looked completely different in ancient times coupled with the chronological change in literary style born out by independant examples. This is where verified research diverges from the previously assumed place-name arguments, assessed on the basis of similarity. This analysis suggests these specific facets of information - an archaeological investigation, historical scrutiny and correct prose structure form a 'palimpsest', when studied enabling a true 'enlightenment' of Egil's Saga.

John R. Kirby
Oxford
25th June 2018

---

[97] Campbell's (1938)
[98] Túlunius (2000, 529)

APPENDIX A - Christian Relationships in Iceland and England (© J. R. Kirby 1999 Oxford).

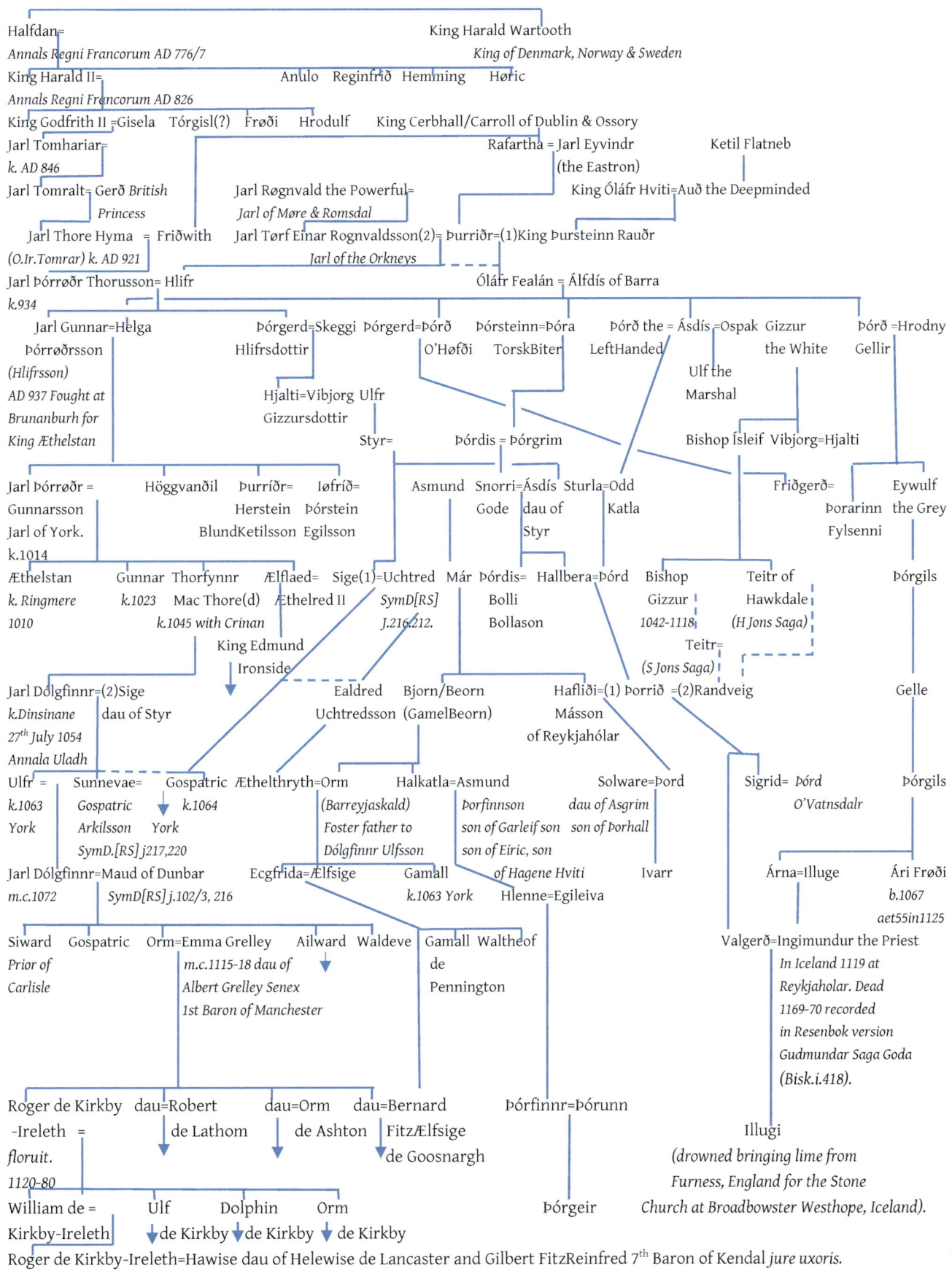

CHRONOLOGY

AD	Events: (plus the chronology of Gunnar's family)	Poets	Egil's Chronology (Scudder)
480	*Dan* stops Caesar *Augustus* at the Limes with a Confederacy of tribes. Nation State of Danmark formed.		
776/7	*Halfdan* brother to *Harald I* Ambassador at *Charlemagne's* court.		
793	First Viking raid on Northumbria		
802	*Harald I* killed at battle of Bravellir	Bragi the Old	
805	*Charlemagne* died ruled for 45 years.		
826	*Harald II Halfdansson* exiled with 400 of his retinue and Baptised at Mainz. Given East Frisia as a fiefdom.		
828	*Godfrith Haraldsson* and his uncle *Horic* try to retake Danmark.		
834	Jarl *Tomhair* killed in battle at Castle Dermot. Jarl *Tomralt* marries *Gerd* a British Princess. Jarl *Tomrar Hyma* marries *Frithwith* dau of King *Cerbhall/Carrol* of Dublin & Ossory.		
850	Beginning of Viking settlement in England from the Great Army.		
870	Beginning of Viking settlement in Iceland		
871	*Alfred the Great* becomes King of Wessex		
885	*Haraldr Harfagri* becomes King of all Norway.	Þjodolfr of Hvinir Þorbjorn hornkloA	
890	King *Þurstein inn Rauðr* killed in Caithness.		
894	*Tørf Einar Rognvaldsson* carves the blood eagle on *Halfdan Longleg*.	Tørf Einar Rognvaldsson	
901	*Alfred* died *Edward* succeeded.		
902	Great fight at the Holme.		902 *Egil Skallagrimsson* born
907/8	Jarl *Þurferth* of Northampton marries *Hlifr* dau of Jarl *Tørf Einar Rognvaldsson* of the Orkneys and Queen *Þurriðr Eyvindrsdottir* widow of King *Þurstein inn Rauðr* King of Southern Cumbria and North Lancashire.		
908/9	*Gunnar Þurferthsson/Þorrøðrsson* born		
911	Kings *Eowils, Healfden*, Earls *Other* and *Scurf*, Governers *Agmund, Othulf, Benesing, Anlaf the Swarthy, Thunferth, Osferth the Collector* and *Guthferth* killed in battle.		
912	*Hrølf (Rollo) Rognvaldsson* Jarl of Rouen is baptised by Bishop of Rouen		
			915 *Egil's* first journey abroad with *Thorolf*
917	Jarl *Þurferth* submits to King *Edward the Elder* Takes an oath to serve him. (A.S Chron).		

AD	Events: (plus the chronology of Gunnar's family)	Poets	Egil's Chronology (Scudder)
925	Æthelstan met *Sihtric* King of Northumbria at Tamworth on 30th January and *Æthelstan* gave his sister in marriage.		925 The Battle of Wen/Vin Heath: *Thorolf* killed
926/7	*Æthelstan* becomes king of Wessex. In this year Fiery rays of light appeared in the northern sky. *Sihtric* died and *Æthelstan* annexed the kingdom of Northumbria. He brought into submission all the Kings of this island. First *Hywel*, king of the West Welsh, *Constantine*, king of the Scots, *Owain*, king Of Gwent and *Ealdred Ealdulfing* from Bamburgh. A covenant of peace established at Eamont Bridge On 12th July. They forbade all idolatrous practices. (A.S. Chron.D).		926 *Egil* marries *Asgerd*
927	*Æthelstan* drove out king *Guthfrith*. (A.S. Chron.E).		927 *Egil* goes abroad with *Thorolf* to Hordaland and north to Sognefjord, then to Courland.
928	*William Longsword* Duke of Normandy succeeds holds Normandy for 15years.		
930	Foundation of Alpingi in Iceland. *Torf Einar Rognvaldsson* Jarl of the Orkneys dies.		
931	*Æthelstan* met with the Welsh at Hereford. They Paid homage to him.		
932/3	*Æthelstan* at York where he occupied himself with his nephew *Louis* and Duke *Hugh* dealing with affairs of state.		
933	*Hakon Godi* (*Adalsteinsfostri*) become King of Norway. Prince *Edwin* was drowned at sea. *William Longsword* becomes Duke of Normandy. Jarl *Þurferth* becomes Jarl of Amounderness under archbishop *Wulfstan I* for *Æthelstan* who gathers a large army.		933/34 *Egils* 2nd journey abroad
934	Jarl *Þurferth* is killed fighting for *Æthelstan* on his Scottish invasion with a land & naval force. (A.S Chron. A)		
934	Jarl *Gunnar Þurferthsson/ Þorrøðrsson* known as *Hlifrsson* in Iceland inherits Amounderness		936/38 *Egil's* 3rd journey
937	Jarl *Gunnar* leads the Christian men of the Danelaw supporting *Æthelstan* at the battle of Brunanburh. *Æthelstan* becomes King of all England, Nation State of England founded.	Gunnar Hlifrsson (uses matronymic)	936 *Egil* meets *Eric* at York 937 *Atli* the short duel with *Egil* in Norway. Went to Iceland that summer- Wintered on the farm.
939	Death of *Æthelstan*.		
939/40	Jarl *Gunnar* goes to Iceland marries *Helga Olafr Fealansdottir*. They have four children *Þorrøðr, Vrai* (known as *Hoggvanðil*), *Þurriðr* and *Iofrið*.		938 This year *Egil* received word from Norway *Eric* had been killed in Britain.

AD	Events: (plus the chronology of Gunnar's family)	Poets	Egil's Chronology (Scudder)
942	*William Longsword* Duke of Normandy dies.		
947	*Eirikr Blodøx* becomes king of Northumbria.		945/7 Egils 4th journey
948	King *Edred* overran all Northumbria because they Had taken *Eric* as their king. Drives out *Eric*.		abroad to Varmland
949	*Anlaf Curran* came to to land of the Northumbrians.		
952	he Northumbrians expelled King *Anlaf* and received *Eric Blodox* the son of Harald.		
954	Northumbrians expelled *Eric* who is killed on Stainmoor.		
956	Archbishop *Wulfstan* of York died 17th Jan.		
958	*Gunnar* comes back to England with his son *Þorrøðr*. Mentioned in various historical charters.		
960	*Haraldr grafeldr* becomes King of Norway.		962 Ode to Arinbjorn
965	Division of Iceland into quarters.	Eyvindr Skaldaspillir	
966	*Þorrøðr Gunnarsson* wastes Westmorland (A.S. Chron). Becomes Jarl of York.	Egil, Kormakr Einarr Skalaglamm	
985	Beginning of settlement of Greenland	Hallfredr	
		Óláfr	985 Death of *Egil*
995	*Olafr Tryggvason* becomes King of Norway.		
999/1000	Christianity accepted in Iceland.	Gunnlaugr Ormstunga	
1000	Discovery of America by *Leif Eriksson*.		
1010	Jarl *Æthelstan Þorrøðrsson* killed at Ringmere		
1014	Battle of Clontarf	Sighvatr	
1015	Nesjarbardagi. *St Óláfr* becomes King of Norway		
1023	Jarl *Gunnar Þorrøðrsson* bondsman for Archbishop *Alfred Puttoc* of York was assassinated at Bath.		
1030	Fall of *St Óláfr* at Stikla(r)staðir	Arnorr jarlaskald	
1036	Death of *Sveinn Knutsson*		
1045	Helganesbardagi. Jarl *Thorfynnr Þorrøðrsson* (*ThorfynnMacThored* - in Manx: *Thorynn*) and *Crinan the Theign* killed by *MacBeth*.		
1046	*Haraldr hardradi* returns to Norway		
1047	Death of *Magnus godi*.		
1054	Jarl *Dolgfinnr Thorfynnsson* killed 24 July at the Battle of Dunsinaine leading the men of Cumbria through Burnam Wood to Dunsinane Hill attacking *MacBeth* from the side with Earl *Siward* and placing *Malcolm III* on the throne of Scotland.		
1056	First Bishop at Skalaholt. *Saemundr inn frodi* born	Pjodolfr Arnorsson	
1062	Battle at Niz / Nissa.		
1064	*Ulf Dolgfinnsson* (the Ailward) & *Gospatric Uchtredsson* (the Ward) murdered under safe passage by *Tostig Godwinsson* at York. Causes the Uprising of the North.		
1066	Fall of *Haraldr hardradi* in England. Battle of Hastings		
1067	*Óláfr kyrri* becomes King of Norway.		
1067/8	*Ari Þorgilsson* born.		

AD	Events: (plus the chronology of Gunnar's family)	Poets	Egil's Chronology (Scudder)
1072	*Dolgfinnr Ulfsson* (fitz Ailward) and *Maud of Dunbar* dau of Earl *Gospatric* of Northumberland & Dunbar marry. *Dolgfinnr* becomes Jarl/Mormaer of Cumbria		
1076	Death of *Sveinn Ulfsson*		
1092	Battle of Cumbria, *William Rufus* defeats *Dolgfinnr*		
1093	Death of *Óláfr kyrri*. *Magnus berfoettr* becomes king		
1095	Death of *Óláfr Sveinsson*.		
1096	Tithe laws introduced in Iceland		
1103	Fall of *Magnus berfoettr*. His sons *Sigurdr*, *Eysteinn* and *Óláfr* become kings of Norway		

BIBLIOGRAPHY

AÐALSTEINSSON, JÓN HNEFILL 1999 *"Religious ideas in Sonatorrek."* Saga-book 25/2: 159-78.

ANDERSON, THEODORE M. 2006 *"Political ambiguities – Egils saga Skallagrímssonar."* The Growth of the Medieval Icelandic Sagas (1180-1280), pp. 102-18. Ithaca and London: Cornell University Press,

ANDERSON THEODORE M. 1994 *"The Politics of Snorri Sturluson."* Journal of English and German Philology 93/1: 55-78.1994

ANNALS OF INNSFALLEN (Unknown author) Ed. Seán Mac Airt. Corpus of Electronic Texts Edition. Funded by University College, Cork and Professor Marianne McDonald via the CELT Project.

ARMES PRYDEN VAWR. (The Prophecy of Pryden the Great), from the *Llyfr Taliesin* (The book of Taliesin) Peniarth MS2 National Library of Wales.

ASHLEY, MICHAEL (1998) *The British Monarchs.* Robinson Publishing.

BAILEY, R.N. & CRAMP, R. 1988 *Corpus of Anglo-Saxon Stone Sculpture Vol. II, Cumberland, Westmorland and Lancashire North of the Sands.* British Academy / OUP pp.150-1.

BANDLE, OSKAR (Ed) 2002 *The Nordic Languages* Handbücher zur Sprach- und Kommunikations-wissenschaft. An International Handbook of the History of the North Germanic Languages.Vol 1. Band 22.1, Walter de Gruyter. Berlin. Pages 824-5, and 832.

BESSASON, HARALDUR 1977 *Mythological Overlays* Sjotiu ritgerdir helgadar Jakobi Benedikisynni Vol 1, pp.273-92. Eds. Einar G. Petursson, Jonas Kristjansson. Reykjavik: Stofnun Arna Magnussonar.

BIRCH, WALTER de GRAY (Ed.) 1885-1893. *Cartularium Saxonicum: A Collection of Charters Relating to Anglo-Saxon History.* Reptd. 1964. 3 Vols. [Vol. 2. pp332-2, Charters 656 & 657] New York and London.

BLANEY, BENJAMIN. 1985 *"The Narrative Technique of Character Delineation in Egils saga Skalla-Grimsonar."* Les Sagas de Chevaliers. Actes de la V. Conférence Internationale sur les Sagas, pp. 343-53. Ed. Régis Boyer. Toulon: Presses de l'Université Paris-Sorbonne.

BREEZE, ANDREW. 1999 *"The Battle of Brunanburh and Welsh Tradition."* Neophilologus 83/3 (1999): 479-82.

BROOKS, W.M. 1885 *The Antiquary: a magazine devoted to the study of the past.* (Oct) Vol XII London: Elliot Stock.

BYOCK, JESSE 2004 *Social Memory and the Sagas: The case of Egils Saga.* Scandinavian Studies 76/3, 299-316.

BYOCK, JESSE. 1986 *The Dark Figure as Survivor in an Icelandic Saga.* In *The Dark Figure in Medieval German and Germanic Literature,* ed. E.R. Haymes and S.C. Van D'Elden. Göppinger Arbeiten zur Germanistik 448. Göppingen: Kümmerle Verlag, 151-163.

CAMDEN, WILLIAM. 1607 *Britannia* (trans.) Philemon Holland.

CAMPBELL, ALISTAIR. 1938 *The Battle of Brunanburh,* London: Heinemann.

CAMPBELL, ALISTAIR 1971. *"Skaldic Verse and Anglo-Saxon History".* Dorothea Coke Memorial Lecture. Viking Society for Northern Research.

CAVILL, PAUL 2008 *The site of the Battle of Brunanburh: manuscripts and maps, grammar and geography.* In a Commodity of Good Names: Essays in honour of Margaret Gelling (eds.) Padel, O.J. & Parsons, D.N., Shaun Tyas, Donington.

CLOVER, CAROL.1978 *"Scaldic sensibility."* Arkiv för nordisk filologi 93 (1978): 63-81.

CLUNIES-ROSS, MARGARET 2005 rept. 2011. *A History of Old Norse Poetry and Poetics.* Pub. D.S. Brewer. 94..

CLUNIES-ROSS, MARGARET. 2004 *Höfuðlausn and Egil's Saga.* Notes and Queries 249 (New Series) 51/2: 114-118.

CLUNIES-ROSS, MARGARET 1989 *"The Art of Poetry and the Figure of the Poet in Egils Saga."* Sagas of Icelanders, pp. 126–44. Ed. John Tucker. New York: Garland.

COLLINGWOOD, WILLIAM GERSHOM 1927 *Northumbrian Crosses of the Pre-Norman Age.* London. Faber & Gwyer. p.54.

COLLINGWOOD, WILLIAM GERSHOM 1895 *Thorstein of the Mere. A Saga of the Northmen in Lakeland.* London: Edward Arnold.

CORMACK, MARGARET. 2001 *Egil's Saga, Heimskringla and daughter of Eiríkr Blódøx.* Alvissmal 10 61-8.

CRAWFORD, BARBARA E. (1987) *Scandinavian Scotland.* Leicester University Press

CRAWFORD, BARBARA E (2004). *"Einarr, earl of Orkney (fl. early 890s–930s)"* [revised opinion AD930].

DE LOOZE, LAURENCE. 1989 *"Poet, Poem and Poetic Process in Egils Saga Skalla-Grímssonar."* Arkiv för nordisk filologi 104(1989): 123-42.

DE LOOZE, LAURENCE. HELGASON, JÓN KARL. POOLE, RUSSELL. TÚLUNÍUS, TORFI H. (Editors) 2015 *Egil the Viking Poet: New Approaches to Egils Saga.* University of Toronto Press. 4:57-75.

DRONKE, PETER.1979 *A note on Pamphilus.* The Journal of the Warburg and Courthauld Institutes. 42, 225-230; see also Dronke 1991 *Latin and vernacular poets of the Middle Ages.* Aldershot.

BIBLIOGRAPHY - continued

DUMÉZIL, GEORGES 1959 trans. 1973 *Gods of the Ancient Northmen.* (ed.) Einar Haugen Centre for the Study of Comparative Folklaw and Mythology, University of California, Los Angeles.III, Cal.371. Translated from G. Dumézil. *Les Dieux des Germains*, Presses Universitaires de France. The Regents of the University of California.

EARLE, J., ed. 1865. *Two of the Saxon Chronicles Parallel with Supplementary Extracts from the Others.* Oxford: Clarendon.

ECO, UMBERTO. 1992 Overinterpreting texts. In Eco, U. Rotty, R. Culler, J. and Brooke-Rose, C. (Eds). *Interpretation and Overinterpretation.* Cambridge, Cambridge University Press. (pp.45-66).

EKWALL, EILERT. 1922 *Place Names of Lancashire* English Series No. XI, University of Manchester.

1936 *The Concise Oxford Dictionary of English Place-Names.* (4th Ed. 1980) Oxford.

EINARSSON, STEFÁN. 1967 "The Poetry of Egill Skalla-Grímsson." Tímarit Þjóðræknisfélags Íslendinga í Vesturheimi 49 (1967): 36-47.

EINARSSON, STEFÁN 1954 "The Origin of Egill's Skallagrímsson's Runhenda." Scandinavica et Fenno-Ugrica. Studier tillägnade Björn Colliander den 22 juli, pp. 54–60. Eds. Dag Strömback, Manne Eriksson, Harald Grundström. Stockholm: Almqvist & Wiksell.

EINARSSON, BJARNI 2003 *Egil's Saga.* Saga Book. Vol. XXVII. Viking Society for Northern Research. U.C. L.

EINARSSON, BJARNI 1974 "On the rôle of verse in saga-literature." Medieval Scandinavia 7:118-25.

EVANS, DAVID A.H. 1997 "Four Philological Notes." Saga-Book of the Viking Society for Northern Research 24: 355-60.

FARADAY, L. WINIFRED. 1906 "Custom and Belief in the Icelandic Sagas." Folklore 17/4 : 387-426.

FARRER, W. & BROWNBILL, J. 1914 *Victoria County History of Lancashire. Vol.VII.* p237.

FICHTNER, EDWARD G. 1982 "The narrative structure of Egils saga." Les sagas de Chevaliers (Riddarasögur). Actes de la V. Conférence Internationale sur les Saga, pp. 355-69. Toulon: Presses de l'Université Paris-Sorbonne, 1982.

FIELD, JOHN 1972 *English Field-Names: a dictionary.* David & Charles: Newton Abbot. p. xiii.

FOOTE, PETER and WILSON, DAVID M. 1970 *The Viking Achievement,* London, Sedgwick and Jackson.

FOOT, SARAH. 2011 *Aethelstan: the first King of England.* Yale University Press: New Haven & London.

FOX, SAMUEL REV. 1864 *King Alfred's Anglo-Saxon Version of Boethius de Consolatione Philosophiae with a literal English translation, notes and glossary.* Bohn Antiquarian Library, London.

GARMONSWAY, G.N. (trans.) 1965 *The Anglo-Saxon Chronicle.* J. M. Dent & Sons.

GUADET, J. (trans.) 1865 *Richer of Riems: Histoire de son Temps Vol 1.* p.125.

GUNNELL, TERRY., 1995 *The Origins of Drama in Scandinavian.* D.S. Brewer – Boydell & Brewer.

GUTHMUNDSSON, BARTHI 1967 *The Origin of the Icelanders.* Trans. & intro by Lee Hollander. University of Nebraska Press.

HALLBERG, PETER. 1968 *Stilsignalement och författarskap i norrön Sagalitteratur. Synpunkter och example.* Göteborg 262.

HALLORAN, KEVIN, 2005 *The Brunanburh Campaign: A Reappraisal,* Scottish Historical Review Vol. LXXXIV, 2: No.218, Oct. 133-148.

HAUGEN, ODD EINAR 2002 95.The Development of Latin Script 1: in Norway. In *The Nordic Languages* Handbücher zur Sprach- und Kommunikations-wissenschaft. An International Handbook of the History of the North Germanic Languages. Ed. Oskar Bandle et al. Vol 1. Band 22.1, Walter de Gruyter. Berlin.

HAUGEN, ODD EINAR 1976 *The Scandinavian Languages: an introduction to their History.* Faber and Faber Ltd.

HELGASON, AGNAR, SIGURÐARDÓTTIR, S., NICHOLSON, J., SYKES, B., HILL, E., BRADLEY, D., BOSNES, V., GULCHER, J., WARD, R., & STEFÁNSSON, K. 2000 *Estimating Scandinavian and Gaelic Ancestry in the Male Settlers of Iceland.* The American Society of Human Genetics Vol. 67, pp.697-717.

HESLOP, Rev. OLIVER. 1892 *Northumbrian Words: a glossary of words used in Northumberland and on the Tyneside.* Vol.1, English Dialect Society.

HILL, PAUL 2004 *The Age of Æthelstan, Britain's Forgotten History.* Tempus pub. (rep. 2011 History Press, p.157-159).

HINES, JOHN. 1994-97 *Egill's Höfuðlausn in Time and Place.* Saga Book Vol. XXIV. The Viking Society for Northern Research. University College London. 84.

HOFFMAN, ANN PRESTON. 2007 "Violence, heroism, and redemption. A study of changing moral norms in five Icelandic family sagas." Ann Arbor (MI): UMI Dissertation Services.

HOLLANDER, LEE M. 1933 "The Battle on the Vin-Heath and the Battle of the Huns." The Journal of English and German Philology 32: 33–43.

JACOBSEN, GRETHE 1978 *The Position of Women in Scandinavia during the Viking Period,* MA Thesis, University of Wisconsin.

JAKOBSSON, ÁRMANN 2015 "Views to a kill, Sturla Þórðarson and the murder in the cellar." Saga-Book of the Viking Society for Northern Research Vol. XXXIX U.C.L.

BIBLIOGRAPHY - continued

JAKOBSSON, ÁRMANN 2011 "Beast and Man: Realism and the Occult in Egils saga." Scandinavian Studies 83/1: 29-44.

JAKOBSSON, ÁRMANN 2003 *Troublesome Children in the Sagas of Icelanders.* Saga Book Vol. xxvii Viking Society for Northern Research, University College London.

JAKOBSSON, ÁRMANN 1999 "Royal pretenders and faithful retainers: The Icelandic vision of kingship in transition." Gardar 30: 47-64.

JAMIESON, JOHN 1841 *An Etymological Dictionary of the Scottish Language.* (Ed.) J. Longmuir and D. Donaldson 1872-82, with supplement 1887.

JANUS, LOUIS ELLIOT. 1994 *The phraseology of Egils saga.* Ph.D. thesis. Minnesota: University of Minnesota.

JOHNSTON, A.W. (July 1916) "Orkneyinga Saga" *The Scottish Historical Review.* Vol. 13, No. 52. p. 393.

JONES, GWYN. 1952 "Egill Skallagrímsson in England." Proceedings of the British Academy 38 (1952): 127-44.

KARLSSON, STEFÁN 2002 *96. The Development of Latin Script II: in Iceland.* In *The Nordic Languages* Handbücher zur Sprach- und Kommunikations-wissenschaft. An International Handbook of the History of the North Germanic Languages. Ed. Oskar Bandle et al. Vol 1. Band 22.1, Walter de Gruyter. Berlin.

KER, NEIL R. 1957. *Catalogue of Manuscripts Containing Anglo-Saxon.* Oxford: Clarendon Press.

KIRBY, JOHN R. 2013 *Early Settlements and their related vills on the Furness Peninsula: Dalton Parish c.AD800-1200.* Unpublished Post Graduate Dissertation, Dept. of Continuing Education, Oxford University, p.27.

KIRBY, JOHN R. 2018 *Identifying Brúnanburh: ón dingesmere – the sea of noise.* Archaeopress.

KRISTINSSON, AXEL 2002 *Sagas and Politics in 13th century Borgarfjordur.* Sagas & Societies. International Conference at Borgarnes. Iceland. September 5-9 2002. Eds. Stefanie Wurth, Tonno Jonuks, Axel Kristinsson. Tubingen: Skandinavistik, Universitat Tubingen. 14pp.

LAUER, PHILIPPE (ed.), 1905 *Les Annales de Flodoard.* Collection des textes pour servir à l'étude et à l'enseignement de l'histoire 39. Paris: Picard.

LINDOW, JOHN 2001 *Norse Mythology: a guide to the Gods, Heroes, Rituals and Beliefs.* Oxford University Press.

LIVINGSTONE, MICHAEL, 2011 *The Battle of Brunanburh: a casebook.* University of Exeter Press. pp. xi-xii.

MAGEOGHAGAN, C. 1627 (trans.) D. Murray 1896 rept. 1993 *Annals of Clonmacnoise* Dublin.

McDOUGALL IAN. 1995 "Discretion and deceit: a re-examination of a military strategem in Egils saga." The Middle Ages in the North-West, pp. 109-42. Eds. Tom Scott, Pat Starkey. Oxford: Leopard's Head Press in conjunction with Liverpool Centre for Medieval Studies.

MORRIS, W. & MAGNUSSON, E.1903 *Höensa Þórirs Saga. (The Saga of Hen Thorir).* Cincinnati, Ohio: Byway Press.

MUIR, TOM (2005) *Orkney in the Sagas: The Story of the Earldom of Orkney as told in the Icelandic Sagas.* The Orcadian. Kirkwall.

NILES, J.D. 1989 *Skaldic Technique in Brunanburh*, in Niles, J.D. & Amodis, M. (eds) *Anglo-Saxon England, Norse-Irish Relations in the period before the Conquest.* Old English Colloquium Series No. 4. University Press of America: Lanham 69-78.

NORDAL, SIGURÐUR. (ed) 1933 *Egil's Saga Skalla-Grimssonar*, Islendk Fornrit ii, Reykjavik.

NORDAL, SIGURÐUR 1953 *Sagalitteraturen.* [Nordisk Kultur VIII: B. Litteraturhistorie. Norge og Island], Stockholm, Oslo, Kobenhavn. 181.

NORDAL, GUÐRÚN 2001 *Tools of Literacy: the Role of Skaldic Verse in Icelandic Textual Culture of the Twelfth and Thirteenth Centuries.* University of Toronto Press.

NORDAL, GUÐRÚN 2001 *Skaldic Versifying and Social Discrimination in Medieval Iceland.* The Dorothea Memorial Lecture. (15 March 2001). Viking Society for Northern Research. UCL.

PAGE, RAYMOND I. 1959 *Language and Dating in OE Inscriptions. Anglia,* LXXVII, p.402.

PHILLPOTTS, BERTHA S., 1920 *The Elder Edda and ancient Scandinavian drama.* Cambridge.

PORTER, JOHN 1876 *History of the Fylde of Lancashire. Fleetwood & Blackpool*: W. Porter & Sons Pub.10-17, 19-20.

POWELL, F. YORK. 1894 "Saga-Growth." Folklore 5/2: 97-106.

ÓLASON. VÉSTEINN 1990 "Jorvik Revisited – With Egil Skalla-Grimsson." Northern Studies 27: 64–76.

RAFN, CHARLES C. 1859 "Connection of the Northmen with the East." Journal of the American Geographical and Statistical Society 1/7: 202-203.

RANKOVIĆ, SLAVICA Ed. 2012, *Modes of Authorship in the Middle Ages.* Papers in Mediaeval Studies 22. Toronto: Pontifical Institute of Mediaeval Studies.

BIBLIOGRAPHY - continued

RANKOVIĆ, SLAVICA and RANKOVIĆ, MILOS 2012. The Talent of the Distributed Author. In Ranković, Slavica ed.2012 Modes of Authorship in the Middle Ages. 52-75 Papers in Mediaeval Studies 22 Toronto: Pontifical Institute of Mediaeval Studies.

ROUGHTON, PHILIP. 2009 *A Hagiographical Reading of Egils Saga*. The 14th International Saga Conference, Uppsala 9th-15th August 2009. Vol. 2. In *Á austrvega – Saga and East Scandinavia*. Eds. Agneta Ney, Henrik Williams and Fredrik Charpentier Ljungqvist in cooperation with Marco Bianchi, Maja Bäckvall, Lennart Elmevik, Anne-Sofie Gräslund, Heimir Pálsson, Lasse Mårtensson, Olof Sundqvist, Daniel Sävborg and Per Vikstrand. Papers from the Dept of Humanities and Social Sciences 14. Institute for Language and Folklore, University of Gävle: Gävle University Press. 2009:816-822.

SAWYER, PETER 1968 *Anglo-Saxon Charters: an annotated list and bibliography*. London.

SMITH, KEVIN P. 1995 "Landnám. The settlement of Iceland in archaeological and historical perspective." World Archaeology 26/3: 319-47.

SPEED, JOHN 1610 *England Part 4: Northern*, Map of Lancashire.

SVEINSSON, EINAR ÓL. 1934 *Laxdaela Saga* Íslenzk fornrit V, Reykjavik.

SØRENSEN, PREBEN MEULENGRACHT. 1993 *Saga and Society: an introduction to Old Norse Literature*. Trans. John Tucker. (Studia Borealia/Norse Studies, Monograph Series I) Odense: Odense University Press.

THORNBER, REV. W. 1837 *History of Blackpool*. Published privately.

TODOROV, TZVETAN. 1970 *Introduction á la littérature fantastique*. Éditions du Seuil, Paris.

TÓMASSON, SVERRIR 2002 *91. The History of Old Nordic Manuscripts I: Old Icelandic*. In *The Nordic Languages* Handbücher zur Sprach- und Kommunikations-wissenschaft. An International Handbook of the History of the North Germanic Languages. Ed. Oskar Bandle et al. Vol 1. Band 22.1, Walter de Gruyter. Berlin. Pp.793-800.

TÚLUNÍUS, TORFI H. 2014 *The Enigma of Egill: The Saga, the Viking Poet and Snorri Sturluson*. Islandica Vol. LVII translated by Victoria Cribb. Ed. P.J. Stevens. Cornell University Library, Ithaca, New York.

TÚLUNÍUS, TORFI H. 2002 "An Attempt at Application: Interpreting Egils saga." *The Matter of the North. The Rise of Literary Fiction in Thirteenth Century Iceland*. Transl. Randi C. Eldevik. Odense: Odense University Press, pp. 234-89.

TÚLUNÍUS, TORFI H. 2001 "The Prosimetrum Form 2: Verses as the Basis for Saga Composition and Interpretation." Skaldsagas. Text, Vocation and Desire in the Icelandic Sagas of Poets, pp. 191–217. Ed. Russell Poole. Berlin, New York: Walter de Gruyter.

TÚLUNÍUS, TORFI H. 2000. *Old Norse Myths, Literature and Society: Saga as a myth: the family sagas and social reality in 13th century Iceland*. Proceedings of the 11th International Saga Conference 2-7 July University of Sidney Centre for Medieval Studies. 526-539.

TÚLUNÍUS, TORFI H. 1994 "The Purloined Shield or Egils saga Skalla-Grímssonar as a Contemporary Saga." Samtíðarsögur. Níunda alþjóðlega fornsagnaþingið. Akureyri 31.7 til 6.8 1994. Vol. 2, pp. 758–69. Reykjavík: s.n.

ÞORGEIRSSON, HAUKUR 2014 *Snorri verses the copyists: An investigation of a stylistic trait in the manuscript traditions of Egils Saga, Heimskringla and the Prose Edda*. Saga Book of the Viking Society for Northern Research Vol. XXXVIII. University College London. 61-74.

VÍGFÚSSON, GUTHBRAND & YORK-POWELL, F. 1905.*Origines Islandicae Vol 1 Landnámabók*. Oxford.

WHITELOCK, D. (ed.) 1955 *English Historical Documents 1, c.500-1042*. London. No. 104

WOOD, MICHAEL. 1980 *Brunanburh Revisited*. Saga Book Vol. XX. Part 3. Viking Society for Northern Research. U.C.L.

WOOD, MICHAEL 2013 *Searching for Brunanburh: the Yorkshire Context of the 'Great War' of 937*. Yorks. Arch. Journal 85, pp138-59.

WYATT, DAVID R. 2009 *Slaves and Warriors in Medieval Britain and Ireland 800-1200*. The Northern World. Brill. Netherlands.